SYSTEMS THINKING
A Guide to Managing
In a Changing Environment

by
Robert Wright

Published by
Society of Manufacturing Engineers
Publications Development Department
Reference Publications Division
One SME Drive ● P.O. Box 930
Dearborn, Michigan 48121

SYSTEMS THINKING

A Guide to Managing In a Changing Environment

TS
176
W75
1989

Copyright © 1989
Society of Manufacturing Engineers
Dearborn, Michigan 48121

First Edition

Second Printing

Library of Congress Catalog Card Number: 88-64038

International Standard Book Number: 0-87263-353-5

Manufactured in the United States of America

To Susie Jean
for the usual reasons —
and for the unusual ones as well

Contents

Foreword

We live in an age of organizations. They are the most pervasive feature of the 20th century. The water we drink, the food we eat, the clothes we wear, and more, all come from our organizations. Without them, life as we know it could not exist. Even the great accomplishments of our era— from space travel to biogenetics—owe their existence to the parentage of productive organizations.

Organizations are more than just pervasive, however. They stand as the most creative and complex inventions of the human mind. Think of the most advanced inventions on earth, such as the super-computers used in scientific and weather research. Complex and creative as these machines are, the organizations that produce them are exponentially more complex and creative. Quoting from an earlier work by Professor Wright:

> "Organizations are the most inventive social arrangements of our age and of civilization. It is a marvel to know that tens of thousands of people with highly individualized backgrounds, skills, and interests are coordinated in various enterprises to pursue common institutionalized goals.*

Organizations are not only pervasive, complex, and creative, they form the foundation and structure of society. The wealth and well-being of society rests squarely on their performance. Comparisons among the countries of the world reveal widely differing standards of living. Some nations—such as Saudi Arabia, for example—are so richly endowed with natural resources that organizations play a small part in their overall wealth. But, a comparison of industrial and past-industrial societies shows the distinguishing characteristic among them to be the relative productivity of their organizations. The more productive their industries become, the more competitive they are in international markets. One need only review the post World War II history of South Korea or Japan to see the electrifying impact of productive industries on their societies' respective wealth and well-being.

With organizations at the core of our lives and livelihoods, organizational productivity becomes the central challenge to those who seek a better tomorrow for themselves and their loved ones. This challenge

---

*Robert Granford Wright, "Managing Management Resources through Corporate Constitutionalism," Human Resource Management, Summer, 1973, p. 15.

leads us, in turn, to the central question facing society today: How do we manage these complex and creative engines of wealth? The very complexity of all but the smallest organizations precludes simple formulae. Even when useful "rules-of-thumb" do exist, their applicability is limited by their simplicity to a narrow range of conditions—conditions that most assuredly will change at an increasing pace in the future.

Systems thinking offers a broad and useful framework for understanding and improving these marvels of the 20th century. It replaces simple axioms with an approach to organizational diagnoses that embrace changing environmental conditions. Change in the organization and its environment can seldom be predicted accurately. What systems thinking gives the manager is a broader perspective, one which considers the changing environment.

Systems Thinking: A Guide to Managing in A Changing Environment explains the systems perspective as applied to organizations. Armed with this understanding, the manager has a fundamental framework for identifying and resolving organizational issues which occur under widely varying conditions.

Within the context of systems thinking, the book goes on to apply various models to the management of production systems. Even for those familiar with systems thinking, the book's application to production offers a variety of unique models and viewpoints from which to better understand complex production systems.

The future prosperity of society and the well-being of its members are intertwined with the fate of our organizations. At the most fundamental level, organizations are a collection of people pursuing organizational and personal goals. The integration of these goals demands that systems thinking be applied to the socio-technical dimensions of organizations. Informed managers applying these concepts can contribute a legacy of productive and humane organizations that shape the well-being of their society.

William B. Werther, Jr., Ph.D.
The Samuel N. Friedland Professor of Executive Management
School of Business Administration
University of Miami
also: White House Moderator on Productivity
and
Senior Moderator at the American Productivity Center

Preface

Certainly I am not as Mahatma Gandhi cautioned, ". . . dreaming of systems so perfect that no one will need to be good." Yet I certainly know that bad systems can make good people behave badly. It is thus incumbent upon designers of others' fates to use sound mental models not only for economic reasons but also for moral ones.

The aim of this book is to provide salient mental models of systems thinking for the practical test of designing the means to accomplish the chores of humankind. It sets forth to provide guidelines to frame questions of design not yet asked, to solve problems not yet faced. Still, the guide does not presume to give patented answers. Rather, it poses models to explore and explain complex organizations—maps to observe behaviorisms and technological territories as they are and maps to plot paths for better ways. The guide encourages its reader, through systems reasoning, to become aware of the multifaceted complexity of highly technical organizations and their management.

The approach of the writing commences with an overview of general systems thinking and then presents components of systems. The reader's attention is then narrowed to the human organization as one, here relevant, species of systems. It is then directed form the abstract "why" of systems thinking to the concrete "how" of operational design. Once designed, attention is turned to the management of a production/operations subsystem, with consideration given to the dynamic interrelationships within the challenges for management to nurture efficiency while also adapting their units to the changing demands of the broader enterprise and its environment. Linkages and interfaces critical to environmental coherence are, in turn, analyzed. Finally the reader is asked to contemplate the consequences of system failures to an individual person and to society.

The promise of this book is that its reader will leave it with a heightened ability to think—in different, more productive ways—about designing and managing technology, culture, systems, people; that is, to orchestrate sound socio-technical systems, especially in a fluid field of environmental forces.

I have often thought—with tongue firmly in cheek—that the delusion of personal intellectual accomplishment forms as one forgets more and more those to whom he or she is indebted for one's own development.

The thoughts in this book stand heavily on the staunch shoulders of countless contributors to my growth; those to whom I am deeply, irrevocably indebted. Though too numerous, and with some too subtle, to mention by name, I acknowledge fully the power of their thinking on my own and hope that I have used it fairly—with their patronage, even wisely.

Robert Wright

Part I

Systems Overview

The study of any system begins with an overview of the creature, thing, or phenomenon one wishes to understand. Later, the pieces can be studied as they relate to each other and the overall picture. The study of socio-technical systems is no exception. **Chapter I** introduces the general field of systems thinking, the essence of the subject. **Chapter II** presents the components of systems, the stuff of which organizational systems are comprised. In **Chapter III,** we narrow our attention to the organization as one type of complex system. **Part I** concludes with **Chapter IV,** which presents specific guidelines for planning and designing socio-technical systems.

Chapter I

Systems Theory

To realize any relations, even if they are correct, is not decisive; what is decisive is that they must be the relations structurally required in view of the whole, arising, conceived, used as parts in their function in the structure. And this holds equally for all operations . . . used in genuine thought processes.[1]

Objectives

To think about systems theory, one needs to develop a certain frame of mind. Most of us have learned to think about ideas, things, and people as static elements compared to and contrasted with each other. Most events that draw the attention of managers, however, are ideas, things, and people in movement together. A person who intends to manage in a dynamic setting needs a new way of thinking about the world. Systems thinking provides the analytical framework for comprehending dynamic, integrated operating situations.

The introductory chapter discusses a useful frame of mind for studying management systems. It defines systems thinking, considers the teachings of general systems theory, and extends the ideas to the design of complex organizations. The objectives of **Chapter I** are as follows:

- To encourage the reader to think in a new way
- To understand the major traits of a system
- To become aware of the different types of systems
- And to learn how systems theory is applied to practical problems.

Introduction to Systems Thinking

We first consider the general value of thinking in systems terms. If we learn what we need to learn, there is little doubt that managers and aspirants to management will see the value of systems thinking. Systems thinking is indispensable to understand, analyze, design, and implement changes in operating relationships. We then establish a brief definition of systems thinking and consider its meaning. Next, examples of varied systems will be presented to clarify the meaning of systems thinking and to extend its use to specific applications.

Value of Systems Thinking

Let us first define a system broadly, yet incompletely, as *any entity— composed of ideas, things, or people—that consists of interdependent parts*. Hence, a group of ideas expressed in prose is a system. A group of things, such as mechanical parts, can make up a system called a bicycle. A group of people forming a soccer team will comprise a system. Once we capture the idea of systems thinking, we can better comprehend a complete array of so-called entities in varied categories in which their overall behavior is influenced by the interdependent actions of parts or people within. We who study systems can be better prepared to explain the behavior of a simple gyroscope or the movement of a complex stellar galaxy.

Systems thinking is a way of reconceiving our experiences. By sensing the interactions of influences in an entity, we recognize that we cannot understand it by simply adding up its parts. We discover instead that it can only be understood by studying the impact of the parts on each other and the net influence of the parts on the overall entity.

For example, systems thinking has the capability to explain widely varied subjects. Its potential value is hardly limited to management systems. Systems thinking helps us to explain other things related to business: The way the economy behaves, how a computer works, or how to use financial data. Beyond studies for professional preparation, systems thinking enriches our personal lives by making more things make sense. And this applies across the board to the chemical, biological, social, economical, political, mechanical, recreational, behavioral, philosophical, and spiritual aspects of our world.

For instance, the casual observer of a professional basketball game may see the replacement of a player, say, Scott for Cooper on the Los Angeles Lakers, simply as a substitution of one guard for another. The experienced coach, however, is anticipating a total change of the interrelationships between the players and, in sum, modified team results. The listener to the Rochester Philharmonic Orchestra who perceives a change of guest conductors from the direction of the late Arthur Fiedler, the venerable master of classical music, to Chuck Mangione, the gifted innovator of jazz music, as only a change of leadership misses the point. The change of leaders is only the catalyst to successive changes that reverberate throughout each section and, in total, impinge on the entire orchestra. Some car owners will replace engine parts intended to boost efficiency, that is, modify performance, only to find that other related parts will not tolerate the increase in power. Those who think in systems terms, however, are aware of the influences of parts on each other and the total engine.

Values can also change the system of one's life. If a person thinks that leisure is good, that value will influence the person's behavior, roles and role relationships, effective incentives, choice preferences—and the overall style of living. As a revealing point of contrast, consider a person who believes that leisure is immoral. Then work that through to its logical impact on the life of the individual. Picture a college student, who, after some false-starts, discovers an exciting career objective for which certain training is required. This source of direction often transforms behavior from half-hearted "intellectual grazing" to behavior marked by self-imposed purpose, dedication, discipline, and zeal to learn. One inspirational discovery can impinge upon the entire system of human behavior and touch nearly every aspect of one's being.

Systems thinking enriches our awareness of nearly all dimensions of life. It explains complexity in a more comprehensive way. Here, cause-effect reasoning alone does not give us satisfactory or useful explanations. Its usual *focus* is on central issues or events. Systems thinking is broadened to the underlying *field* where issues and events begin. Through this focus-field approach, we can understand both what is happening and, more valuably, *why* it is happening.

In a more dramatic way, systems thinking offers a new and better method for dealing with the great challenges, problems, and opportunities facing society. The further advance of this new style of thinking is the most significant prediction that can be made about coping with the future.

> The new style of dealing with the future has no accepted, inclusive name, but the names of its more highly developed techniques have become familiar in the last ten years to most businessmen, government officials, military officers, scientists, and technicians. The techniques themselves are apt to be called "systems analysis" or "systems planning."[2]

5

Systems thinking is now widely used to solve problems of universal significance. It is immensely valuable here in a number of ways: First, systems thinking classifies projects; second, it draws together authorities from varied disciplines to work on projects; third, it integrates the total body of knowledge needed to work on a certain project; and fourth, it candidly recognizes that in worldly progress the end is inseparably bound up with the means.[3]

A Definition of a System

By classifying a word through definition, we find that new ways of thinking are opened to us. We hope that such an expansion of thought processes will be brought about here. Earlier we defined a system roughly as "any entity—composed of ideas, things, or people—that consists of interdependent parts." At that point, a partial definition was adequate to introduce systems thinking. Here, however, a fully developed definition of a system is required so that specific examples can be considered.

> A system is an identifiable, complex dynamic entity composed of discernibly different parts or subsystems that are interrelated to and interdependent on each other and the whole entity with an overall capability to maintain stability and to adapt behavior in response to external influences.

By that definition a universe of things, ideas, and people can be called systems. And, indeed, we would be correct in believing that nearly anything that deserves our attention is a "system"—whether it be a physical, biological, social, or management system. Let's now dissect that definition and see what it tells us.

Identifiable. A system has definable boundaries and is thereby recognized as a composite of things. It differs from its setting. A system is not an unorganized, randomly scattered clutter in some field of environment. It is cohesive, identifiable, and unique.

Complex. A system, as Webster informs us, is a whole made up of complicated and interrelated parts. Systems study deals with intricate and involved things, the very things that most of us study hard to comprehend. A system is not a set of simple and unrelated stuff.

Dynamic. A system is marked by motion. It is dynamic. It is through movement that a system's parts become interrelated and can interact. Even when a system is in a stable state, such as a galaxy, a clock, or a human organization, the system has motion within. When a system stops functioning and becomes static or still, it ceases to be a system. It either becomes a framework, or it ceases to exist. A mechanical engine meets the definition of a system when it is running. When turned off, the parts and overall machine become a structure. A human organization is a system. Yet, when it no longer functions, it ceases to exist.

Entity. A system is an entity which includes anything that is distinctive, either fact or thought. For instance, the biological system of a rose or the mechanical system of a drag race car is a fact. The system of ideas that interweave to make up a philosophy or poem form a thought. An entity, as you can see, can be very specific and concrete. It can also be very general and abstract. Entities that are systems in fact form a span from one extreme to the other. We should be aware of all the entities that form the hierarchy because we may in time want, or need, to evaluate any one of these sets of facts or thoughts.

Discernibly Different Parts or Subsystems. A system contains more than a single aspect. It is made up of a set of structures—physical, mechanical, biological, or ideological—where each structure can be identified and where each structure is unique. Thus, a car engine has discernibly different parts—such as an alternator, a carburetor, and a water pump—each an element of a subsystem. In this example, the alternator is a part of the electrical subsystem, the carburetor a part of the fuel subsystem, and the water pump a part of the cooling subsystem. The reader will notice that subsystems are usually composed of a number of parts. The electrical subsystem is made up of such parts as the battery, relay, spark plugs, and wiring, together with the alternator. A subsystem is thus formed. When the subsystems for power, fuel, electricity, temperature regulation, and so on are brought together, they form the car engine system.

The car engine referred to above as a single entity is called a *system.* When combined with the other parts, with body, chassis, suspension, and so on, the engine becomes a *subsystem* of an automobile system. When cars are combined with other modes of travel, they form a transportation system. A single car is now only a subsystem. When the transportation system is then seen as a part of the economic system, transportation becomes a subsystem. This reasoning can of course be broadened to the super system under which all lesser entities are subsystems.

The fact that all systems, except one super system, are but subsystems is a critical observation. It teaches us to sense relativity.

Interrelated and Interdependent. Parts or subsystems work together and depend on each other They are neither capable of working alone, nor of functioning without the support of the overall system. The

7

example of the car engine is again useful here. Each subsystem—electrical, fuel, and cooling—is related to and dependent on the others. Further, each subsystem is dependent on the overall engine for its power source, structure, and maintenance.

Overall Capability to Maintain Stability. A system has structure for patterned behavior so that it demonstrates stability and continuity. It uses inputs called resources to sustain itself. These resources may be fuel, heat, air, protein, or other inputs depending on the type of system. When we refer to stability, we mean that the system attains a steady state *in its environmental field and internally.* But a steady state does not mean static. All systems are dynamic within, as mentioned. For instance, even at rest, the human body functions at a low ebb.

Adapt Behavior in Response to External Influences. A system is able to change to ensure its survival as external changes occur. This means that it must be receptive to external influences, be able to translate data, and be willing to respond. Adaptive behavior has two forms: the first form is merely to react to outside forces; the second is to proact to impending forces. Reactive adaptation is passive, proactive adaptation is active. External influencers refer to forces beyond, or outside, the definable boundaries of a system. Part of the resources attracted to the system are used for adaptation, either reactive or proactive.

In Summary. That gives us a working definition of system. Though not universally accepted as the only way of defining the term, it helps us to narrow the study. It is useful because it points out the sweeping applications of systems thinking. It helps us to better understand varied entities—the universe, a philosophy, a government, an organization, a plant, a family, or other phenomenon.

Examples of Systems

If someone asked "Is 'enterprise' a system?," how would you respond? With that handy variety of true–false question, you would touch the word "enterprise" against your newly-found definition of system and respond, "yes." But, let's imagine that the questioner probes further and asks, "why?" It is now helpful to make certain what the other person means by the word "enterprise," if a bothersome, unproductive analysis and response is to be avoided.

Enterprise can refer to "free enterprise," an economic and political philosophy that underlies the market mechanism of a number of nations.

Now, are you correct with the "yes" answer? Sure. It is a free enterprise system because it meets the definition of a system in all ways. It is a clearly differentiated type of economic activity, moving with parts or subsystems that include government, financial, and business enterprise functioning in tandem, and with the overall subsystems adjusted to be consistent with the overall economy. It can be maintained in a reasonably stable state without erratic swings from uncontrollable inflation to deep depression. But it must also adapt to influences such as foreign economies and politics, rates of exchange, devaluations of monies and tariffs.

"Enterprise," the questioner imposes, could also refer to the U.S.S. Enterprise, an aircraft carrier. Would you now be correct with the "yes" answer? Of course. A carrier is an integrated system that meets the definition. It is certainly identifiable. The carrier is vibrantly in motion with mutual dependence upon subsystems, such as power, communication, weapon defense, steering, and navigation. It is a stable entity, yet its behavior is adaptive to the broader efforts of the fleet and its mission.

So far, so good. Your affirmative response continues to stand correct. But would you lose a bit of confidence if the questioner responded "No, what I had in mind was the spacecraft named 'Enterprise' in the television series, Star Trek?" Is it a system? If so, why? Your batting average of correct responses can now soar. "Absolutely," you respond. The spacecraft meets all of the criteria of a system, with subsystems for such functions as thrust, navigation, and life-support, all interdependent on and interrelated to each other and to the spacecraft as a whole. It adapts to such external forces as gravity, heat, and density in the environment of space.

Finally, the fellow reveals that "Enterprise" is the surname of a person. Now, you cling solidly to your original "yeh," but here you note ". . . perhaps the most complex of all systems." Right again, without question. Each of us is a system, an exotic one with a plethora of interactions. Consider, for simplicity's sake, merely the physiology of a human as a system. Indeed, a human is highly individual and complex. Subparts link to form identifiable processes such as skeletal, digestive, circulatory, respiratory, glandular, and excretory subsystems. Each is related to and dependent on the other and the overall physiology of the system. A human is equipped with a finely-tuned sensory subsystem. Changing external conditions such as temperature, moisture, sound, and light are instantly perceived and processed. And, in turn, behavior is adapted to ensure the well-being and survival of a human being.

9

You did well in the true–false quiz by scoring perfectly. Yet people often do well, given a chance (say, 50/50) on that type of exam. Now consider specific systems in which you may have an interest. Apply the guidelines of general systems theory to those systems as you read on.

General Systems Theory

The broad way of thinking under which more narrow systems studies take place is called General Systems Theory. It serves as a framework under which we use generally accepted guidelines to study specialized subjects such as the organization systems, management systems, and production/operations systems described in this book. General Systems Theory is known by its initials GST (which, pleasingly, does not form an acronym).

We touch on the overall field primarily to gain a historical perspective of GST. We should also form an idea of the reason the Theory is needed, especially for those persons studying a discipline as complex as organization and management. To gain those advantages, let us look briefly at the origin, reasons for development, major traits, and strengths and weaknesses of GST.

Origin of GST

In a certain sense, systems thinking is as old as recorded history; in another sense, it is a very young science. Pre-Socratic scholars of the sixth century B.C. learned to find and consider an order, or *kosmos,* that was cohesive, intelligible, and controllable by thought and action. Many of the great discoveries were made possible because adventuresome intellects broke with the then popular, but static "gear-theory" of their times, when cause-effect analysis grudgingly provided enlightenment step by step. Systems thinking underlies massive intellectual contributions such as Copernicus' explanation of astronomy, Newton's laws of motion, Darwin's thesis on natural selection, Harvey's theory of blood circulation, and Freud's contribution to psychiatry. Each man contemplated his field of study in a systems way before guidelines for general systems theory were formed.

The ideas behind GST are attributed to the German philosopher, Georg Wilhelm Friedrich Hegel (1770–1831):

1. The whole is more than the sum of the parts.
2. The whole determines the nature of the parts.

3. The parts cannot be understood if considered in isolation from the whole.
4. The parts are dynamically interrelated and interdependent.[4]

Though many of Professor Hegel's other views now stand discredited, his "new Logic" initially became a useful way for biologists to study living processes where an analytical-mechanistic approach is impossible.

The 1930's and 1940's were marked by an outcry for a newer, more advanced logic capable of embracing studies of both nonliving and living things. Unlike studies of nonliving matter where closed systems theory may be used, inquiries into living things require open systems theory for analysis. In a closed system, no exchange takes place with the outside; with an open system, exchange does take place. Further, as studies move from physical and mechanical to biological, social, cultural, and ideological systems, they become progressively more complicated. The plea was responded to in 1950 by the father of GST, Ludwig von Bertalanffy and by a small group of brilliant, dedicated pioneers whose papers preceded or confirmed Professor von Bertalanffy's views.[5]

In 1954, the Society for General Systems Research was founded. Under the leadership of biologist von Bertalanffy, its membership included economist Kenneth Boulding, biomathematician Anatol Rappoport, and physiologist Ralph Gerard.[6] These men formed the nucleus of a school of thought whose time had come.

From that beginning, GST can now be looked on as a conceptual revolution. Drawing heavily on biology, mathematics, physiology, and economics, GST has been extended to many fields. The growth of the use of GST has been impressive. At a recent meeting of the Society for General Systems Research, to illustrate the sweeping interest in GST, such varying applications as humanism, behavioral change, philosophy, curriculum, aeronautics, esthetics, neurons, and, of course, management systems were discussed.

Reasons for Development

GST was originally developed to solve a specific problem: There was no analytical "systems map" to fully explain organic biology. As with management systems, it deals with varied principles and with systems at all levels. Biology is also concerned with subparts and subsystems affecting each other and the overall organism. That was the dilemma.

The biochemists did not conclude, [however] because the methods used in the analysis of simple inorganic compounds would not work in dealing with complex organic substances, that therefore no adequate methods were possible. . . . On the contrary, they went ahead to invent new methods as well as new techniques for the understanding of organic part-whole relationships.[7]

In the same way, we who aim to understand management and organization must adopt a systems approach to master our inquiry.

GST, however, gives us more than an analytical framework. It seeks to find methods of solution to problems in one type of system and extend the methods for use on other types of systems. Systems theorists combat narrowness, so that they can generalize their findings to related problems in other unrelated systems.

One of the most pervasive appeals of GST was stated well by Professor John A. Beckett, management scholar and consultant on systems design:

The thrust of general systems might be described as an effort to bring together various approaches to the field of reality, to take advantage of the qualities of each, and perhaps to add new dimensions. It is not quite enough to say that the search for general systems principles raises the sights of scientific inquiry from parts to wholes; it also draws attention to the study of relationships of parts to one another within the wholes and recognizes that when a new entity is added to . . . any system, not only are new relationships of all old entities with the new entity involved, but [also] new relationships among all the previously existing entities may be created.[8]

GST thus provides an analytical framework which can be applied to differing types of systems. It further encourages us to understand relationships within systems more clearly.

Major Traits

GST is a young science in its current state of application. It therefore has little unquestionable doctrine. As the most abstract of all systems theories, the traits attributed to it are many. But the traits that follow are generally conceded to be the major benchmarks of GST *beyond* those basic traits included in the earlier definition.

   1. Goal Seeking. A system's inner actions result in some position of dynamic equilibrium where activities can be directed to goal attainment. The goal may be outer-directed to an environmental end or inner-directed to maintain and perpetuate the life of the system.

2. **Holism.** A system is an inseparable entity. Hence, each one requires study as a whole or study holistically. (Please don't ask what happened to the "w". Not even Webster knows.) If one tries to dissect a system, interactions crucial to understanding are lost. A study of the heart, for instance, explains structure but its functioning can be understood only when it is analyzed as a part of circulation and overall physiology. The logician Sir Arthur Eddington put the matter simply and squarely before us when he wrote: "We often think that when we have completed our study of *one* we know all about *two,* because 'two' is 'one and one.' We forget that we still have the study of 'and.' "[9] GST is consciously concerned with Eddington's "and."

In another way, holism applies a Gestalt approach by viewing a whole entity with all its parts in natural motion.[10] It does not force divisions of the indivisible that erroneously stop the system's inevitable movement. Again, we point out that a GST approach provides a field-focus viewpoint. The relevant field is first studied, then we narrow our focus to the part of specific concern.

3. **Hierarchy.** A system has subparts or systems that are nested in a ranking, or hierarchy, from those of major importance to the success of the system down to those subsets of only minimal influence on goal attainment. For instance, in a certain manufacturing plant where processes are highly mechanized, subsystems for the technology, raw material flows, and machine maintenance are essential over less sensitive subsystems. By contrast, in a plant where the work is largely conducted by skilled craftspersons, subsystems of labor and organization would be critical to success, with other subsystems following in a descending order of importance.

4. **Inputs and Outputs.** A system is dependent on resources from its external environment. In closed systems, the resources needed are prearranged and supplied before the system is sealed from outside forces. Their goal is merely self-maintenance, or their output is stored within the closed system. A perpetual motion device, some mathematical expressions, self-winding watches, or perhaps the solar system, are examples of *relatively* closed systems. Nearly all systems attracting extensive

study are open systems. Here, inputs flow into the systems and outputs emerge from the systems over their entire life cycle.

5. **Transformation.** A system converts inputs into outputs after some modification of the inputs is made by the system. The form of outputs is different from the inputs, both as individual inputs and as collective inputs.

6. **Energy.** A system gathers and/or generates energy. This trait is not commonly mentioned; yet the notion is significant. A system gets needed energy as an input, or by generation within, or from some combination of these sources. Conventional forms of energy include electricity, protein, gravity, steam, pumps, or generators. These are inputs that provide a physical or biological system with the means to function. GST, however, also explains the behavior of human, social, political, and ideological systems. Less conventional, but indispensable, forms of energy are also needed for the support and output of these types of systems. The forms of essential power are assertiveness, influence, or spirit, from either people or ideas. They are inherent powers in some systems. The implications of the need for these forms of influence should be of special interest to fellow students of leadership.

7. **Entropy.** When a system runs down or reaches a condition of maximum disorder, we say it is caused by entropy. It was adopted as a factor to measure the unavailable energy in thermodynamic systems.

A system tends to degenerate. In closed systems, this occurs when they use up resources, or the system wears out. In open systems, entropy is not automatic because they have continuing supplies of inputs or resources. Yet the tendency for degeneration is still there. One explanation has to do with the use of resources affecting output. An open system uses resources in two ways: To produce output and to maintain itself. It could easily become entropic if an unreasonably high proportion of its energies were consumed by its needs for self-maintenance, to the neglect of producing a sufficiently high output. For instance, if a social system called a school with a mission (output) of teaching somehow removed its best teachers from the classroom and into administration or research (self-maintaining pursuits), entropy could set in, as its primary mission was eased out.

Entropy is also seen to occur when a system is unable to generate enough energies within. Another reason given is when subparts or subsystems merely wear out, if not maintained or replaced.

Whatever the causes, a system tends to be influenced by a limited life cycle. During its formation and maturation, it gathers power. In its declining era, it tends to dissipate power or to use its energies poorly, at times to the point of ultimate inertia. At that point—inertia—the system is transformed to static structure and this occurs with mechanical, biological, social, religious, and philosophical systems.

8. **Equifinality.** This cumbersome word simply means that an open system can reach its goals in a number of ways. This flexibility on the means to goals is made possible because, unlike a closed system with a pre-set alternative, open systems can change inputs and some can also change goals. Hence, the tendency toward entropy, if not toward inertia, can be thwarted by open-systems when they can be managed.

When one contemplates the nature of systems—their definition and major traits—it is at times useful to consider them as they relate to some system quite familiar to you—yourself, your family, a car, a social organization, or a business enterprise. Often, the new concepts of GST acquire real meaning when applied to some entity near (and perhaps dear) to the reader.

Problems and Strengths

Any new way of thinking is beset by problems when we first try it. The use of GST is no exception to that rule. Though the use of systems reasoning expands our horizons of knowing, its use commands an intellectual, and/or perhaps more dear, a psychological price.

Problems. First, by encouraging us to consider a broader view, GST takes from us (at least, initially) the comfort of mastering details. Some people find this discomfort too costly. Second, to understand systems, one must be content to understand relationships instead of absolute facts. Professor William Wolf, the provocative management scholar, stated the dilemma nicely when he wrote:

A major problem inherent in [the use of systems theory to explain organization behavior] is that one must accept a concept of relativity that is tremendously complex and, when followed through logically,

15

leaves one with little firm ground upon which to stand. Absolutes vanish, and events and happenings have to be explained in relation to other aspects of the situation.[11]

The fear that the use of GST will end with *only* the conclusion that everything is somehow related to everything else is a real concern for some designers.

This drawback is especially serious for those who need the precision of cause-effect analyses. "Causal thinking," as Professor Angyal, a noted psychologist, observes "has been used . . . for such a long time and, in certain fields, with such success that it is almost generally considered as *the* scientific thinking."[12] Though some readers will feel more comfortable and will accept more readily analyses of stimulus-response, that type of analysis may well be only a sub-variety of GST. Nevertheless, some will reject systems analysis in favor of detailed examination because they cannot purposely think without a problem to solve. A note of optimism should be sounded here to relieve such anxiety.

The relatively vague initial conception of the total system is transitory. As a general understanding of the overall system is attained, the student can then narrow the analysis to details, *but with an overall understanding in mind.*[13]

Other problems involved with the adoption of GST are those with dual objectives: ". . . optimization vs. suboptimization, idealism vs. realism, incrementalism vs. innovation, agreement vs. consensus . . ."[14] and we might quickly add, theory vs. practice.

Strengths. First, GST has potent unifying powers. It promises to provide a single language and a single set of laws for many studies. If so, we need not fall into the trap of earlier specialists who found no common ground for intellectual exchange. Where,

. . . physicists only talk to physicists, economists to economists— worse still, nuclear physicists to nuclear physicists, and econometricians to econometricians. One wonders, sometimes, if science will not grind to a stop in an assemblage of walled-in hermits, each mumbling a private language that only he can understand.[15]

Indeed, science or practice can ill-afford single-talented isolationists. Business, indeed, finds them intolerable. Management is deeply involved in and widely concerned with varied thinking. Myopia here is deadening.

Second, GST gives us the potential to understand functioning organizations of matter, people, events, ideas, and happenings. If we study the parts or subsystems alone, we will lack knowledge of the whole entity.

If we study the overall entity without comprehending its makeup, this also fails to give sound awareness. GST frees us from the parts-versus-whole dilemma.

> Every time that any elements whatever, in combining release new phenomena by their combination—it is necessary to think of these phenomena as situated not [only] in the elements but [also] in the whole formed by their union.[16]

All designers expect to learn their chosen fields of study. For business designers, among others, the immediate field they should expect to learn—organizational systems and their broader environments—can be mastered only with the help of GST.

Levels of GST. We have seen that GST goes beyond any single study. Herein is one of its major strengths. There are a number of levels of complexity and abstraction from the lowest level where static structures are studied to the highest level of unknown absolute truths.

Let's review the entire hierarchy of complexity. To do so, we use the most frequently cited array of types of systems developed by a pioneering general systems theorist, Kenneth Boulding. First, an overview of the entire hierarchy is useful (Figure I.1.) We can then learn about the nature of each level of the hierarchy and move to an analysis of the application of GST.

Level 1, Frameworks. Static structures make up this most elementary level. One must be able to cope with frameworks such as the skeleton, the set of stars, and the formal organization before moving to dynamic behavior. By our earlier definition, frameworks would not be included as a system.

Level 2, Clockworks. The simplest of dynamic systems are included here, such as machines, the solar system, and of course, clocks. Movements are predetermined by functional need. The theories of physics and chemistry rest within level 2 where systems are essentially closed.

Level 3, Cybernetics. At this level systems become more open. There is feedback from the environment so that the equilibrium of the system is self-regulated within certain limits. No feedback on control is built-in, however, to change goals. Such systems as thermostats and maintenance of body temperature belong here. Cybernetic systems belong to areas studied by the engineer, computer specialist, and biologist.

Level 4, Open System. The fourth level of systems includes those with the capacity for structural self-maintenance by transforming material and energy. At this level, elementary forms of life are introduced.

High Level

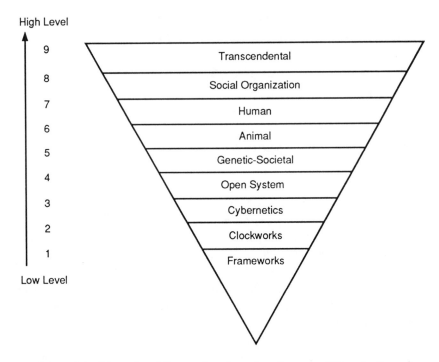

9 Transcendental
8 Social Organization
7 Human
6 Animal
5 Genetic-Societal
4 Open System
3 Cybernetics
2 Clockworks
1 Frameworks

Low Level

Figure I.1. Hierarchy of System Levels ased on Degrees of Complexity and Abstraction

Indeed, it was called the "level of the cell" and attracts the scrutiny of biochemists.

Level 5, Genetic-Societal. At this level, cells are specialized and structured with information receptors. Yet the living system is not refined to a point where it can process and react to, in any great degree, received data. The system's life stages are prescribed genetically. This is the level of plant life where botanists pursue their studies.

Level 6, Animal. At this level the living system is mobile, goal-directed, and self-aware. It can receive, process, store, and respond to external information. As the scale of animal life is ascended, behavior is caused not merely by stimulus-response, but rather by stimulation—"image"—response.[17] The animal can determine certain goals and means to goals within bounds imposed biogenetically. Animal systems—which are considerably more complex than lower levels—are studied by zoologists, ethologists, and biogenetic theorists.

Level 7, Human. In addition to possessing all of the *traits of animal systems,* humans are complicated by their ability to think about the future, set goals, and plan to reach them. Humans are self-reflective—they not only know things, but also they *know* they know things. Human systems are further complicated by advanced images, symbolism, symbolic interpretation, and language. Man—marked off in many ways from less-gifted animal brethren—commands great interest from man. He is studied from all vantage points by students in many disciplines.

Level 8, Social Organization. The social organization level builds upon and includes all of the complicating features of human systems detailed in Level 7 [as those aspects in the Human level (7) encompassed those elements in the Animal level (6)]. Humans form organizations of humans. These are called social systems. They are important because they include humans and surround humans. Organizations include many subsystems, among them values, norms, and roles. These open systems are studied by all social scientists.

Level 9, Transcendental. Level nine is different from previous levels of systems. It kindly allows for future discoveries of the now unknown. These findings will include the discovery of ultimate truths and these absolutes must of logical necessity form a systematic, organic structure. Once found, we will be able to see clear relationships between the subsystems of the known, and this, *the categorical system.*[18]

Application of GST

Let us now consider several examples of the use of GST. One does not have to look far to see systems at work to serving man, such as health care, delivery systems, fire protection systems, banking systems, defense systems, and product-producing systems. We will present certain applications of GST here that are less commonplace, more curious.

First, imagine a plant that produces nylon hosiery sitting alone on a plot of desert land. No employees work here. The production system is run almost exclusively by high-speed, automated equipment. The system is open but by only a minimum degree. It is opened to its environment to receive inputs of energy, raw materials, and computer instructions from a person at a far-distant point. It is opened to permit the finished nylon products to be taken to markets. Here, then, is the application of GST, essentially, at the levels of clockworks and cybernetics.

Next, envision a broader application of GST used here to monitor the supply of growing food worldwide. The system is needed to assure an adequate supply of food to decrease shortages. It is especially valuable to developing nations that have insufficient data for forecasting the production of agricultural products. To monitor agricultural growth, orbiting satellites gather the basic data. It is relayed to the latest generation of computer to be processed and analyzed as it relates to foods stored (overproduction or deficits), other sources of protein, imports and exports, and of course demand for food. Then, all reasonable options are evaluated (scanned) by the system to alleviate any shortages or to use surpluses. The monitoring reports, theoretically, could then be transmitted by the satellites to the nations' leaders. This application of GST merely extends our human and cybernetic capabilities to an open communications system. (Now, if we can only convince some people that when we monitor silos, we are concerned specifically with grain storage, we might get the system off the ground.)

Finally, imagine a system designed to solve man's earthly difficulties with environmental limitations, over-pollution, over-population, and under-supplies of energy. These are the problems that Princeton physicist Gerald O'Neill put squarely before his students—together with the idea that a space colony orbiting at a point called L5 by scientists could circle the earth for eternity. Under O'Neill's guidance, the students produced a prototype of a space colony. Unlike science-fiction fantasy, the National Aeronautics and Space Administration is taking the project rather seriously. The construction of the colony uses a provocative innovation,[19] but the design of social support systems represents the boldest and most imaginative uses of GST.

Each space colony can support 10,000 inhabitants through integrated subsystems essential to a human world (on paper—a more human world). Its economic subsystems would produce and transmit power, purify pharmaceuticals and crystals, and gather ore-rich asteroids, all for use on Earth. The colony's social and political subsystems would be experimentally derived with the technological option of a semi-closed community of 10,000 people. The agricultural subsystem would produce wildly with nutrient-enriched moondust in environmentally controlled "pods." New sports, arts, and recreational subsystems would spring forth at areas in the colony yielding spacelike weightlessness.

Earth's first space community—about a quarter of a million miles away—would entail "the creation of a [semi] closed ecosystem with its complex interactions of chemicals and organisms."[20] Whether the space colony becomes a reality or not, the processes used by its planners demonstrate the remarkable potential of GST.

Summary

For a designer, systems thinking provides a broad analytical framework to understand dynamic operating situations. It provides a new way of thinking that can enrich our awareness of all aspects of life. The definition of a system alone indicates the versatility of systems thinking.

General systems theory (GST) serves as the broad framework under which organization and management systems are studied. It was developed precisely for use by those persons in dynamic fields of operation. The traits discovered in GST are the same as those found in organizational systems, and its subsystems for production/operations, marketing, and finance. Though its use demands certain intellectual and psychological adjustments, it is the only known way to make sense out of complexity. GST, once mastered, has far-reaching potential to serve mankind.

Notes

1. Max Wertheimer, *Productive Thinking* (New York: Harper and Brothers, 1945) p. 43.
2. M. Ways, "The Road to 1977," *Fortune* (January, 1967), p. 94.
3. *Op. cit.,* p. 197.
4. D. C. Philips, "Systems Theory—A Discredited Philosophy," *Abacus* (September, 1969), pp. 3–15.
5. John P. Van Gigch reports in his *Applied General Systems Theory* text (New York: Harper & Row Publishers, 1974, p. 50) that, although Bertalanffy's paper was most important to GST, the following scholars made valuable fundamental contributions: Koehler, Redfield, Singer, Sommerhoff, von Neumann, Shannon, Weimer, and Ashby. Ludwig von Bertalanffy, "The Theory of Open Systems in Physics and Biology," *Science 3* (1950), pp. 23–29; W. Koehler, *The Place of Values in the World of Fact,* (New York: Liveright, 1938, reprinted in F. E. Emory (ed.), pp. 59–69; Robert Redfield (ed.), *Levels of Integration in Biological and Social Systems,* (Landcaster, Pa.: Jacques Catell Press), "Introduction," reprinted in Buckley (ed.), pp. 59–68; E. A. Singer, "Mechanism, Vitalism, Naturalism," *Philosophy of Science 13* (1946), 8199; G. Sommerhoff, *Analytical Biology,* (London: Oxford University Press, 1950), excerpt reprinted in Buckley (ed.), pp. 281–295; John von Neumann, "The General and Logical Theory of Automata," in Lloyd A. Jeffress (ed.), *Cerebral Mechanisms in Behavior: The Hixon Symposium,* (New York: Wiley, 1951), reproduced in part in Buckley (ed.), pp. 97–107; C. E. Shannon and W. Weaver, *The Mathematical Theory of Communications,* (Urbana, IL.: University of Illinois Press, 1949); Norbert Weiner, *Cybernetics,* (New York: Wiley, 1948); see also Weiner's *The Human Use of Human Beings,* 2nd ed., (New York: Doubleday, 1954); and Ross W. Ashby, *Introduction to Cybernetics* (1956) and *Design for a Brain* (1954), both published in London: Chapman & Hall.
6. Peter P. Schoderbek, Asterios G. Kefalas, and Charles G. Schoderbek, *Management Systems: Conceptual Considerations,* (Dallas, Texas: Business Publications, Inc., 1975), p. 8.

7. Harold A. Larrabee, *Reliable Knowledge* (Boston: Houghton Mifflin Company, 1964), p. 340.
8. John A. Beckett, *Management Dynamics: The New Synthesis* (New York: McGraw-Hill Book Company, 1971), p. 62.
9. Sir Arthur Eddington, *The Nature of the Physical World* (Ann Arbor, Mich.: The University of Michigan Press, 1958), pp. 103–104.
10. Schoderbek, *et al., op. cit.,* p. 13.
11. William B. Wolf, *Management: Readings Toward a General Theory* (Belmont, Calif.: Wadsworth Publishing Co., Inc., 1964), p. 326.
12. A. Angyal, *Foundations for a Science of Personality* (Boston: Harvard University Press, 1941), p. 261.
13. Robert Granford Wright, *Mosaics of Organization Character* (New York: Dunellen University Press of Cambridge Series, 1976), p. 117.
14. van Gigch, *op. cit.,* pp. 34 and 35.
15. Kenneth Boulding, "General Systems Theory: The Skeleton of Science," *Management Science,* April, 1956, p. 198.
16. Emile Durkheim, *Les règles de la mèthods sociologique,* 2nd ed. (London: Allen and Unwin, Ltd., 1927), p. XV.
17. Richard A. Johnson, Fremont E. Kast, and James A. Rosenzweig, *The Theory and Management of Systems,* 3rd ed. (New York: McGraw-Hill Book Company, 1973), p. 9.
18. Boulding, *op. cit.,* pp. 197–208, for the hierarchy, but the author is responsible for interpretations of Boulding's work within each level.
19. For further discussion, see Ron Chernow's "Colonies in Space May Turn Out to be Nice Places to Live," *Smithsonian,* April, 1976, pp. 62–68.
20. *Op. cit.,* p. 68.

Chapter II

Components of Organizational Systems

A system is a configuration of components interconnected for a purpose according to a plan.[1]

Objectives

To comprehend organizational systems and how to design them, a manager needs to be acquainted with the conditions that influence their configuration and operation. The designer is guided thereby to be aware of what influences can be changed, what influences cannot be changed and must be therefore reflected in the organizational design, and those conditions that impose inviolable organizational imperatives. Stated another way, those who will build organizations must know what influences they can change, what conditions they must live with, and those elements essential to the survival of the unit designed.

Chapter II prepares the reader to comprehend the complexity of socio-technical systems—part human, part machine. It discusses the societal field of organizational systems, internal components, and ends with a definition of an organization, based on the definition of general systems presented in **Chapter I.** The goal here is threefold:

- To portray the field with which organizations must interface
- To discuss the components of organizational systems
- To present a definition of an organizational system.

As the reader may sense, we are moving inward from the presentation of general systems to influences on the design of organizational systems. We will in turn narrow our exploration further to the design of organizational systems, and finally confine our attention to the design of production systems.

Field of Organizational System

Systems components depend on their field, or domain.[2] The field influences the configuration of a system.

In the study of biogeography, for example, land masses or whole continents are characterized by clear divisions of territorial life zones called biomes. Some of the biomes recognized by ecologists are tundra, coniferous forests, deciduous forests, subtropical forests, grassland, desert, chaparral, and tropical rain forests. In each biome the kind of vegetation is uniform—grasses, trees, cactus, and so on—depending on the physical environment. These two factors of the field—biome and vegetation—combine to determine the kinds of animals present, which must be supported by the biological field.[3] If we are studying the animal life as living systems, the field is the biome. In this illustration, the animals as individuals, or as populations, are symbiotically dependent on the field of their physical environment because they lack the means to change it.

Organizational Systems

A human organization exists in a field of influences that, to a degree, support it and shape it; and to some degree the field is influenced by the organizational system. The production system of a company, for instance, acquires resources from the broader organization, is designed to some high measure to produce what products or services marketing and engineering propose as lucrative, and in turn, can influence the field of functional divisions by demonstrating its capabilities and expertise. Thus, a *mutual influence* prevails.

This mutuality of influence occurs for three reasons. First, there is a mutual dependence between institutional systems and their environmental field. Second, organizations are *concentrations of power* sufficiently open to make their influence felt. And third, *equifinality* unlocks organizations from pre-set destinies, so that their leaders can change things—goals, means to goals, inputs, and to some degree, elements in their organizations' environmental fields.

Environmental Influences

By "environmental influences" we mean those conditions that affect the organization or the results of its action.[4] As here used, the environment is not thought of merely as the context of organizations. Instead, the environment represents a field of forces, or potential forces, to which the organization must be sensitive enough to "hear" and resilient enough to adapt. Adaptation, as has been discussed, may take the form of changing internally, or it may take the form of changing an environmental influence.

The overall organizational system is influenced by the following classifications of forces or potential forces:

Constituent Groups. These are the groups of people who support the enterprise, such as shareholders of businesses, patrons of museums, donors to charities.

Groups Served. These are the groups of people who benefit from the products or services produced by an enterprise, such as customers of businesses, visitors to museums, and receivers of charity.

Industry Customs and Traditions. Organizations in different fields, sometimes classified as industries, are bound to certain behavior culturally. For instance, electronics firms are commonly innovators, banks are usually conservative, and oil companies are historically adventuresome.

Technology. The state of the art of making things, more often the changing state, acts as constraint and opportunity. Though some technological advances are generated within organizations, many others are foisted upon the enterprise by outsiders, such as research laboratories, equipment manufacturers, governmental agencies, and occasionally, university professors.

Economy. Organizations adapt to economic conditions since no single organization can substantially alter such things as the supply of capital, its cost, the rate of inflation or deflation, the state of employment, or disposable personal income.

Values, Mores, and Ethos of Society. These factors are the underpinnings and causes of certain human behavior. If, for instance, great numbers of people harbor a serious concern over the growth of population and become content with smaller sizes of families, the resulting demographic trends and life style could alter the types of products and services that appeal to them.

Public Opinion. Organizations must bend to the aggregate of public sentiment, especially when it reflects deep feelings of support for something or rejection of something. As examples, if public opinion swells for clean air, a copper company must respond in a constructive way rather than dismissing the plea by blaming others for contamination. If, on the other hand, public opinion has been caused to grow to reject persons in authority positions as cheaters and liars, leaders of organizations would be wise to take advantage of every opportunity to restore the faith in leadership.

Political Trends. The political winds, and in turn the governmental agencies they impact, blow in varied directions over time, both domestically and internationally. In one span of time, nationalism seems preeminent; in another period individual rights take precedence. The political breezes waft between conservatism and liberalism, a laissez-faire attitude to direct involvement in organizations of all kinds. Organizations must react, either by acquiescing to the prevailing conditions or by initiating or supporting a countervailing political philosophy.

Legal Climate. In a land of law, neither individuals nor organizations of individuals are above it. They must be sensitive not only to the legal climate, but also to the changing interpretations of laws.

Markets. Organizations are dependent on their environmental field for all of the resources required for their functioning, such as workers, managers, capital, land, equipment, and materials. The availability and cost of each of these classifications of resources, or inputs, are governed by the mechanisms of each one's particular market. Leaders of enterprises keep attuned to these various markets to anticipate what means will be required to attract essential resources and to estimate the costs attendant on their use.

An organization as an active system will attempt to reach out and give order to its complex environmental influences so as to cope with them effectively. As the organization grows and specializes along the lines of functional subsystems, it also segments its environmental forces into related sectors.[5] Traditionally, industrial organizations become segmented into the three essential subsystems of sales, research and development, and production.[6] Each of the basic three subsystems (among other specialties today) "listens" to environmental data that will influence its specific operations. Although through this process we gain the benefits of specialists receiving specific data, some external data must be integrated because it will have an impact on the overall organization.

Components of Organizational Systems

In **Chapter I** we analyzed the major benchmarks of General Systems Theory (GST) to better understand the lessons provided by this fledgling science. GST told us that most systems are goal seeking, holistic, hierarchical, deal with inputs and outputs, transformation, energy, entropy, equifinality, and servosystems. We can now apply these elusive ideas from GST to the more meaningful design of an organically sound organization.

Goal Seeking

The design of an organization, as with most systems, is securely anchored in goals, or common purpose. Human organizations as open systems have explicit outer-directed, environmentally-directed goals and an implicit, inner-directed, goal of self-perpetuation. As you will recall, both types of goals use an organization's resources. The need for self-maintenance cannot be permitted to divert an excessive amount of resources from production.

Holism

An organization is a cohesive organism of inseparable activities, functions, and subsystems. Our focus is the organization. Its external field provides the broader support, or maintenance systems. When we are thinking about total organizations, this field is sometimes referred to as the *ecosystem.* When the forces from the ecosystem grow unfriendly, even threatening, an organization tends to become more cohesive.

Hierarchies

Organizational arrangements are based on hierarchies of goals, structures, and plans. The key point here is that these hierarchies must be designed to "fit" the organizational mission and the nature of the participants in the enterprise.

Inputs and Outputs

An organization, unlike preprogrammed, closed systems (e.g., a self-winding watch), is an open system that uses inputs from its environment. These inputs, sometimes called *factors of production,* include such resources as people, land, money, machines, equipment, and management.

Further, an organization is considered to be an open system because it is also dependent on its environment to use its outputs of goods and services. And this fact holds true for whatever it produces—athletic events or tires, jazz music or backpacks, charitable help or recreational vehicles.

Transformation

Organizational systems attract inputs, or resources, and transform them into products or services. For instance, a chair manufacturer transforms wood, doweling, varnish, and so on into completed pieces of furniture through the use of craftspeople, management, and machines. In another way, a professional football team transforms individual players and fields of play (play?) through coaching and management into powerful entertainment for sport fans.

The end product or service provided therefore differs from the elements that were used in its formation. With business organizations, there is an *added economic value* brought on by the transformation, so that revenues gained from sales are greater than the costs of inputs, thus producing profits. With nonbusiness organizations, the transformation ostensibly brings on *added social value* in such forms as parks, museums, charities, and national defense. In production, the process of transformation is often called *conversion*.

Energy

All systems attract energy from outside or generate energy from within. Human organizations use various conventional forms of energy. They also have the ability to generate power inherently from the assertiveness, influence and spirit of their members.

Entropy

Closed systems tend to degenerate automatically, to use up resources, to run down. Open systems, like organizational systems, need not automatically degenerate because by their open nature they can regenerate—replace worn equipment or obsolete thinking. Organizations historically tend to have a limited life span, however, even though their potential is timeless.

Equifinality

Closed systems have a prearranged manifest destiny in the fulfillment of their missions, only one way of reaching it. Organizations, as open systems, are capable of changing inputs, the conversion process, subsystems, and indeed, goals. However, applying this invaluable capability of flexibility to ensure survival depends on the willingness and ability of leaders to bring on desirable changes—to consider other ways, to entertain new ideas, and to listen to discontents.

Servosystem

A servosystem is an automatic control system designed so that output can be constantly or periodically compared or contrasted with inputs through feedback. By using a servosystem in an organization, differences between the two quantities or qualities can be used to analyze the causes of variances and to bring on the desired performance. A servosystem is an extension of the idea of using some servomechanism for control.

In Figure II.1, Worker/Organization Productivity Servosystem, we can see a model designed to illustrate the way factors interact to influence worker performance. The designers of the servosystem have kept the level of detail to a manageable level, while making it sufficiently thorough to possess both conceptual meaning and practical use. Here are the authors' instructions for the use of this particular component:

> Individual worker performance is shown as the focal point of the model; organizational and individual factors either directly or indirectly impact this performance. Any factor shown in the model can be traced through the model as an input to worker performance. In fact, many factors also can be traced to performance as an output. Because of this feedback effect and the time delay characteristic, the model has been labeled a servosystem.
>
> Factors are indicated in the model in several different ways. First, individually-controlled factors are distinguished from organizationally-controlled factors. Second, factors that may be changed significantly only in the long run are identified separately. Third, some factors serve to control the rate of transfer of one or more of the other variables. Fourth, the model includes time as an implicit factor since the feedback would take place over time. The time factor is also explicitly included by the time delays shown at a variety of places in the model. These delays indicate the changes in the factors to which they relate will affect performance rather gradually over time. Fifth, the "Factor Interaction" block indicates that "Functional Effort" of individuals is a rather complex phenomenon that is more than a simple addition of the levels of the factors that are direct inputs to the individual.

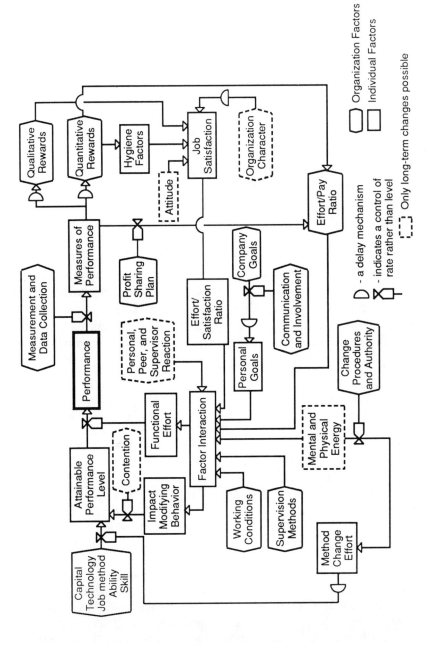

Figure II.1. Worker/Organization Productivity Servosystem. (Source: William A. Ruch and James C. Hershauer's *Factors Affecting Worker Productivity*, Bureau of Business and Economic Research, Arizona State University, 1974.)

30

The servosystem model of worker/organization productivity is based upon research from an extensive review of related literature and information gathered during visits with several productivity conscious organizations. In addition, the modeling procedures of industrial dynamics have guided the form used.

The model is intended to provide a theoretical foundation for understanding and analyzing worker performance. In addition, it is hoped that the model will serve as a practical guide to organizations in determining how to improve productivity and in evaluating the relative impact on worker performance of changes in certain factors.

Evaluating the impact of instituting special programs to affect performance or satisfaction is a particularly useful feature of the model because of the large number of such programs that are thrust at organizations.[7]

The servosystem model shown in Figure II.1 is a comprehensive schematic of the overall production system intended to analyze the factors affecting the performance of the individual worker. Other servosystems could be designed to evaluate the influence of precise subparts of the system. Or, a servosystem could be designed to *systemically monitor* some crucial subsystems within a production function, such as quality assurance, scheduling, or personnel turnover. Indeed, the servosystem component of organizations has widespread, perhaps sweeping, application in all functional areas.

Definition of an Organizational System

In **Chapter I** we considered a general definition of a system so that we could gain an understanding of varied applications of this way of thinking. You may recall that you were asked to apply the definition to the word "enterprise" merely to suggest the broad application of systems thought. You might recall further that whether the word "enterprise" meant an economy, an aircraft carrier, a spacecraft, or even a person with that name, each could be viewed as a system—philosophical, mechanical, and psychological, respectively. Now, let's apply the definition to a human organization so that you can gain a first-estimate of what is involved in designing and managing an organizational system.

Here is the definition introduced in **Chapter I:**

A system is an identifiable, complex dynamic entity composed of discernably different parts or subsystems that are interrelated to and interdependent on each other and the whole entity with an overall capability to maintain stability and to adapt behavior in response to external influences.

The definition was broad to encourage general application. Now, we will apply it to overall organizational systems and later to the production system. Let's again dissect that definition, but here to better comprehand its influence on the design of organizations.

Identifiable. An organization is cohesive, not an unorganized clutter of randomly occurring events. Indeed, the word "organized" has grown to mean a coherent pattern of behavior of something or someone. For Webster, the antonym of system is "chaos."

An organization is unique with its own particular image, personality, or character. When you think of Sears, it is somewhat different from Penney's, as is the Red Cross from the Salvation Army, or the musical group E. L. O. from the BEEGEES. And this identifiable quality holds even when two or more organizations have the same mission. This trait has caused people to observe that a specific organization is to an extent:

1 like all other organizations
2 like some other organizations, and
3 like no other organization.[8]

Though we will here be examining how organizations are "like all other organizations," we should be aware that on-going, functioning units—whether overall organizations or production systems—develop their own unique identity.

Complex. An organization of people, together with their technical and economic trappings, is not simple to understand. It is intricate and involved. It is thus worthy of study since those who master it are rare and valuable to themselves and others. But remember that a social organization is at level eight of complexity on Boulding's nine-level hierarchy of systems.

Comprehending human organizations, however, is not as difficult as trying to understand the random, sometimes capricious, behavior of individuals. Organizations move rationally to reach enterprise goals. (Or at least when viewing models of highly desirable organizations, that's what we should find.) Hence, grasping models of sound organizational behavior is always easier than comprehending random behavior.

Dynamic. An organization churns with activity, a series of events that give it a pulse-like tempo. In the illustration of the car engine used earlier, we found that when it is turned off it ceases to be a system and becomes a physical structure or framework. When an organization is "turned off" because of the end of a scheduled shift, a holiday, or a shutdown for retooling for a new product design, it is reduced to an image, rather than a structure, until it resumes operations. For example, when Chevrolet shuts down to retool for a model change, called changeover, the organization in production ceases to exist. Even the organization's structure disappears temporarily. Though it is nonexistent, we still have the illusion of Chevrolet's bustling assembly plant though it defies observation.

The dynamics of human interaction add to the complexity of designing and managing an organizational unit—and to the real challenge. The well-known organization chart with its lines and boxes is a static simplification of the way an organization should work. Because it cannot portray the dynamics of things, according to a respected colleague, it's about as useful for explaining organizational life as the drawing of a stick man for human behavior.

Viewing the dynamics of organizations another way, imagine yourself comfortably settled on a platform of a tower overlooking a marshalling area on which a military unit is standing in customary regimental formation. You sense immediately the authority structure because you can discern the ranks from commanding officer, through platoon leaders, to squad leaders, and finally, to squad members. Indeed, if somethow the formation could be made vertical, rather than horizontal, with the commanding officer on the highest plane sequentially to squad members on the lowest level, you would be viewing a typical formal organization chart. Whether on the field or somehow suspended, the unit is merely structured. Only when the top leader barks the order to fulfill some mission do you witness the organization as an intensely dynamic one in which highly pitched interaction displaces the symmetry of formalized arrangements. Structure has been converted to a system.

Entity. Since it is identifiable with boundaries between the organization and its environment, we refer to the system as an entity. The abstract term well suits the definition of an organization because, though it may be intangible, it exists as surely as does a car engine.

Discernibly Different Parts or Subsystems. An organization involves more than a single aspect, such as a paper clip or piece of pencil lead. In total, an organization has sets of structures including goals, plans, and formalized organizational arrangements, such as job descriptions, methods, and a formal organization chart. In addition, the total organization has subsystems for technical, economic, physical, behavioral, and managerial requirements. For example, a disco place requires the technical subsystems of equipment to reproduce music and to provide refreshments, the economic subsystem to ensure a sufficient flow and stock of funds, the physical subsystem to make entertainment or dancing enjoyable both functionally and aesthetically, the behavioral subsystem so that employees demonstrate suitable roles, norms, and values as hosts, and the managerial subsystem that will identify the jobs of employees, maintain communications, reward desired performance, and control performance that damages the enterprise. (A system. Remember?)

An overall organizaton has functional subsystems all related to the whole. We have been led to think of these subsystems as structured divisions or departments. In reality, they are subsystems. Subsystems for such functional specialties as personnel, engineering, production, finance, and marketing.

Within the overall organization there exists a system to produce a service or product. It might be called customer service, accounts payable, auditing, or production, depending on the type of company. Viewed from the top of these production units, each one—whether it produces a tangible good or an intangible service—is a system. Typically, each production system will have essential internal subsystems for such requirements as job design, inventory control, quality control, and production control. And within, each of these subsystems has desirable, discernable subparts and subsystems.

As with GST, which has a hierarchy from complex and abstract levels of systems down to relatively simple and concrete ones, organizations contain varied levels of complexity and abstraction.

Interrelated and Interdependent. All segments—parts and subsystems—of an organization depend on each other to move the system toward its goals. They are as incapable of functioning alone, or without the support of the broader organization, as are the subsystems of the car engine example used earlier. Each subsystem of the engine, as you will recall—electrical, fuel, cooling, and so on—is interrelated with and interdependent on each other and the broader vehicular system. Each subsystem of an organization—work processes, authority, incentives, control, and so on—are similarly dependent on each other and the overall framework of the organizational system. Viewed in this coherent, interactive way, one can sense that when things are designed and managed properly *a balance is maintained.* Conversely, when internal arrangements are tinkered with without understanding their intimate interaction, organizational imbalances surely will occur.

Overall Capability to Maintain Stability. An organization demonstrates the capability for continuity, an orderly pattern of stable behavior within. Organizations use resources to sustain themselves and to produce something. These inputs include money, machines and equipment, management, labor, raw materials, and miscellaneous supplies and services. Organizations provide output that includes goods and services to users. The inputs and outputs of organizations represent major influences from the environmental fields of organizations. When we consider organizational stability, we mean that the organizational system can reach a steady state *within its environmental field and internally.* This requires the use of the field-focus approach discussed in **Chapter I.**

Stability in organizations is required to achieve high productivity by efficiently using, or employing, costly resources (inputs). An organization that is unable to maintain stability, at least in the short run, will also be unable to attain efficiency. By "efficiency", we mean here maximizing outputs of products or services with inputs of resources limited by their cost. It is a ratio of outflow related to inflow. As an example, the Chevrolet Division of General Motors presumably must change models annually to respond to consumer desires. The instability caused by the yearly changeover is within tolerable economic limits. If however, Chevrolet tried to change models monthly, the cost of the instability created would be prohibitive. In an organization, the degree of stability allowed is limited by the rate of changes taking place in the environment.

Adapt Behavior in Response to External Influence. An organization ensures its survival by being able to respond appropriately to external forces in its environmental field. This requirement implies that its leaders must be attuned to outside influencers, be able to translate relevant data, and be willing to respond. Forces that impinge on organizations and require responses include social, economic, political, legal, and technology aspects, presented earlier.

Some systems are unable to react. The old car engine cannot adapt its behavior to meet new needs for efficiency and environmentally acceptable performance. Indeed, it may be incapable of even being modified, and thus, need to be junked. Other systems are able only to react. A shore bird can adapt only within narrowly genetically defined limits to the effects of pollutants in its environment. While other systems—man and his/her organizations—have the adaptive capability both to react to environmental conditions and to change certain of those conditions.

Either form of change within a human organization however, is active not passive. That is, an organization faced with, say, a change in affirmative action legislation may decide to (1) only minimally comply with the law, (2) do what other organizations are doing, or (3) launch programs to change conditions in a positive way well above legal requirements and industrial precedent. Whether a reactive or proactive strategy is adopted, active changes by leadership must be taken. Passive waiting leaves the leadership outside the law and the organization vulnerable to damaging litigation and accompanying notoriety.

Part of the resources of the organization—human, technical, financial, or whatever—are used for *adaptation.* Others are used for *self-maintenance,* e.g. certain internal communications, rituals, and ceremonies. While still other inputs are marshalled for *production* of goods and services. All three uses of resources are essential to long-run survival of an organization. However, systemically-caused imbalances among the three can easily occur, and become malfunctional. This potential problem deserves a closer look later in this chapter when we explore the organic makeup of an organization and its implications for managers.

Efficiency can be achieved only through stability, as we've said. However, being able to adapt to external forces is crucial to long-run survival. Management, as has been observed often, involves the ability to create stability amid change, and to cause change amid stability. It's a matter of relativity that is sensed by the leaders of successful organizations. Too much change is damaging—too little change is deadening.

This presentation shows the way the general definition of systems applies to organizational systems. It should be noted that unlike systems governed by physical or natural laws, organizational systems must be managed by men and women if they are to be productive, yet resilient and self-renewing. The application of systems theory to organizational systems gives us an acute awareness of the challenge for leaders.

As we narrow our viewpoint from general systems theory to organizational systems theory, we see that organizations are but a special type of system—a social system—with particular, sometimes subtle, but always important distinctions. Let us now consider a definition of a sound organizational system:

> An organization is an open social system of coordinated activities by two or more participants designed and managed to pursue a goal(s) through subsystems internally consistent with each other and its goals, while adjusting to maintain environmental consonance.

In the upcoming passages of this book let us construct an ideal organization, from its beginning elementary framework to its final complex form. To do so, let's first consider its hierarchies, its basic structural/functional form, its internal organic subsystems, and finally, the organization's external environment.

Organizational Hierarchies.[9] Each organization has structured hierarchies explicitly stated or implicitly agreed to that convey what its leaders wish it to do and how they want it done. By hierarchies, we mean that leaders classify in ranks *goals, plans,* and *organization structures* from general guidelines to specific prescriptions.

The design of an organization is based on its hierarchy of goals—on what it is trying to achieve. Goals come from an assessment of opportunities and restrictions in the environment. Once goals are set, they point out the functions to be fulfilled by people within pursuit of enterprise goals. The organizational hierarchy is built as a reflection of goals. Next, a hierarchy of plans is designed as the means to encourage organizational participants to pursue overall goals in an orderly way. These plans range from broad policies and strategies down to specific rules and routines, from broad guidelines at the top to specific instructions for operating individuals at the bottom.

These hierarchies—goals, organization, and plans—are depicted in Figure II.2. They communicate achievements required and role expectations in such a way that they are meaningful at each authority level,

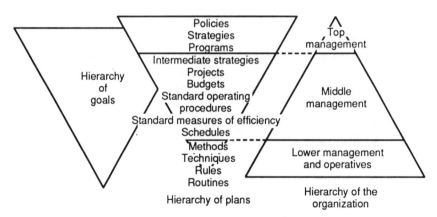

Figure II.2. The Relationship of the Organization to Hierarchies of Goals and Plans. (Source: Adapted from Robert Grandford Wright, "The Myth Inherent in Responsibility Center Management, MSU Business Topics, Spring 1972, Vol. 20, No. 2.) (Used by permission of the publisher, Division of Research, Graduate School of Business Administration, Michigan State University.)

from top management to the lowest operating position. Thus, an inverse relationship emerges between the hierarchies for goals and plans and the organizational hierarchy, as Figure II.2 depicts.

Further study of the Figure reveals that broad plans—policies, strategies, and programs—give top management adequate guidance for making decisions and taking action. However, it will also become apparent that these plans are too general to provide sufficient direction to lower-level managers and workers. They require the more finely detailed directives provided by methods, techniques, rules, and routines. The hierarchy of plans serves to form essential subsystems, e.g. work processes, incentives, and control.

Here, we have discussed structural hierarchies in the overall organization. It should be carefully noted that hierarchies for particular activities are essential to the efficient operations of subunits of the overall organization—in such units as finance, personnel, marketing, engineering, and production/operations.

Summary

Many of the teachings of systems theory can be used by the student of management to design sound socio-technical systems. By understanding the conditions, components, and nature of organizations, one gains the ability to sense imperatives, responsibilities, constraints, and opportunities available to the architect of systems created by man.

To develop this valuable ability, we presented the idea of human organizations as a partial product of a field of external forces with which they must interface. The major environmental forces were detailed. Next, we considered certain of the components of organizational systems—the way in which systems thinking is translated and applied to the practical art of designing organizations. The components include the concepts of goal orientation, holism, hierarchies, inputs and outputs, transformation, energy, entropy, and servosystem.

We then developed an operating definition of an organization based on general systems precepts (GST). As we narrow the focus of our thinking from the consideration of GST inward to a view of organizational systems, we find that they are but a special type of system—a socio-technical system—with special applications of systems theory and distinctive implications for designers and managers.

Notes

1. Mel H. Grosz, Internal Memorandum, Esso Mathematics and Systems, Inc.
2. John P. Van Gigch, *Applied General Systems Theory,* (New York: Harper and Row, Publishers, 1974) pp. 39–47. Through presentation of the domain and properties of general systems.
3. Claude A. Villee, *Biology,* (Philadelphia, Pennsylvania: W. B. Saunders Company, 1962), p. 586.
4. F. E. Emery, ed. *Systems Thinking,* (Middlesex, England: Penguin Books Ltd.), p. 155.
5. William A. Ruch and James C. Herschauer, *Factors Affecting Worker Productivity* (Tempe, Arizona: Bureau of Business and Economic Research, Arizona State University, 1974) p. 34 and p. 36.
6. *Op. cit.*
7. *Ibid.*
8. Chris Argyris, *Diagnosing Human Relations in Organizations,* (New Haven, Connecticut: Yale University Press, 1956), p. 17.
9. Robert Grandford Wright, "The Myth Inherent in Responsibility Center Management," *MSU Business Topics,* Spring, 1972, Vol. 20, No. 2.), pp. 49–58.

Chapter III

Organizational System

Artificial systems are designed to fill basic needs and perform crucial functions—stability, viability, communications, divisions of labor, and coordination—analogous to those carried on by natural systems.[1]

Objectives

The purpose of organizational systems is to achieve the goals of man—political, economic, spiritual, or whatever—that are beyond the reach of any individual person. Organizations are the means to do the large jobs of society. Therefore, the vitality of a society depends on the strength of its organizations, in addition to the well-being of its individual citizens. Indeed if individuals are to be effective, their ability to do so is usually bound up with the effectiveness of the organizations in which they play various parts.

Unlike natural physical and biological systems, human organizations are created and managed by men and women. Good organizations are designed by using the guidelines provided by systems theory. The objectives of **Chapter III** are the following:

- To be aware of the requirements of an organization
- To apply systems concepts to the design of organizations
- To gain a conceptual overview of the systemic nature of organizations
- To understand the life cycle of an organizational system

What Is an Organizational System?[2]

When a person begins nearly any study, there is a need to define the topic being explored. Curiously, when one has progressed to advanced study, he or she feels compelled to again define the topic. So, contemplate the nature of an organizational system with us. It is somehow different from a group of people. But in what major ways does it differ? Is a neighborhood an organizational system? Is a political party? A class of students? A cocktail party? A business? A faculty? A church? A marriage? Each assemblage, quite frankly, could be a group, an organizational system, or even disorganized anarchy. It depends on the application of systems theory that can give it coherent structure. Let's now analyze certain qualities of organizational systems that separate them from human groups.

Goals

Most people would agree that an organization must have a common purpose, whereas a group need not identify jointly adopted goals. This means that an organization has *its* goals and that its members agree to contribute in their way to the attainment of those goals. Indeed, as participants in organizations identify with organizational goals and become dedicated to them, a more unified, cohesive, and aspiring force is marshalled. Dedication to a common mission may come forth naturally in organized efforts with compulsive persuasions, such as for charitable, religious, service, social, or political purposes. However, in the many organizations where emotional appeals are absent (such as, for example, the production of pickles), *other means are required to engender commitment.* This crucial aspect of an organization will be probed a bit later.

Formal Structure of the System

Common pursuits alone do not require organized human efforts. A class of students, a group at a party, a faculty of teachers, or even partners in marriage will have common purposes; but many goals may be reached independently, that is, without a structured pattern of expectations and behavior among participants. Thus, an organization forms when there is a common purpose, or purposes, that require *coordinated activities* by two or more participants to achieve the goal or goals.

A formalized structure, or patterning, of events and happenings is designed to prolong continuity of effort over time and to reduce haphazard, or random effort. Specialization, job descriptions (roles), job responsibilities (norms), groups of classifications, leadership, specialized staffs, and a hierarchy of authority forms a structure. Then, as authority to act is delegated, the social structure is transformed from a static set of fixed relationships among participants into dynamic interaction between mutually dependent members. In this manner, a functioning organization is born.

Complicating Features

To this point, we have recalled the rudimentary elements of a human organization—goals of the organization and organizational members placed in logical hierarchical relationships to pursue those goals. So far, our definition essentially echoes Chester I. Barnard's observation from the late 1930's: "a formal organization is a system of consciously coordinated activities of two or more persons."[3] But does Barnard not extend the definition? Thus far, our elementary model of an organization deals only with goals and people positioned to reach them. Barnard dealt with efficiency of human effort when he inserted the qualifying phrase, "consciously coordinated" before the word "activities." Efficiency—maximizing output as it relates to inputs—must expand the basic model of organization if the system is to socially and/or economically justify its existence. This would explain the design approach to organizational systems. An accomplished designer would insist upon efficient design with the following phrase: An organization is a goal-seeking social system, but if it is to be efficient, its subsystems must be designed and calibrated to fit each other and, in concert, move the people in the social system toward the enterprise goals. Stated concisely, an authority in systems design would insist on a condition of *internally consistent* subsystems.

We would also be reminded that an organizational system depends upon its external environment for its survival or long-run effectiveness. The organization, as a social entity, is an open system that exchanges matter, money, products, ideas, services, beliefs, and people with its environment. And it *must* continue to do so to exist. Let us limit our concern here to the vital element of people as they relate to the open nature of organizations.

People (their hopes, skills, fears, knowledge, foibles, beliefs, and all) are attracted to an organization when trade-offs are desirable to them. People who "fit" remain; those who do not "fit" do not stay. People leave the organization for other opportunities; people retire; people are demoted and promoted; people disassociate from enterprise goals, but some remain on the payroll; people die. The influence from this specific form of openness causes changes in two ways: First, an organization's productive capabilities change with the changing composition of its people, and second, its ability to maintain its strengths changes as its people change.

Most important here, the *open* quality of organizations means that they must continually assess conditions in the external environment and respond appropriately. In the area of personnel, there is a need to reassess changing expectations by prospective employees on incentives, work demands, personal growth, and so forth. The labor market, used as an example, is but one narrow aspect of environmental forces. But it illustrates the point that organizations must be receptive to external forces and responsive to those forces urging change. An organization needs to be in phase with its broader support system if obsolescence is to be avoided. Briefly stated, a sound enterprise is *environmentally consonant*. This requirement further expands the conditions that prevail in a model of a sound organizational system.

Here, then, are the major components of the conceptual overview of the organization; it must include: Common Purpose; Social System; Internal Consistency; Environmental Consonance. We can now consider the relationships of these varied components of organizational strength and their implications for systems designers.

The Conceptual Overview

The conceptual overview provides a valuable vantage point for students of organizational design. First, it encourages one to get out of the organization, to hold it at arms length, and to view its overall makeup. Second, it provides a framework for the organic segments of organizations as they should be designed, that is, as an ideal model. Next, it illustrates the logical flow of change, from the environment, to goals, to the social system, and to internal subsystems. Finally, it diagrams the definition of a sound organizational system repeated here as it was presented originally in **Chapter II.**

> An organization is an open *social system* of coordinated activities by two or more participants designed and managed to pursue a *goal or goals* through subsystems *internally consistent* with each other and its goals, while adjusting to maintain *environmental consonance*.

The model is presented to illustrate the way organizations should work, with varied integral elements in balance. In this way, the conceptual overview is like the macro economic model advanced by Keynes to illustrate full employment equilibrium, with inflation, recession, and depression representing departures from that desirable state. As with the Keynesian model of a sound economy, a sound organization moves toward a point, or range, of equilibrium with its functional areas and subsystems in reasonable balance. An organization, somewhat like the larger economy, can be permitted to go flat, to be depressed, so that stagnation sets in with eventual obsolescence and ultimate demise. In the other extreme, an organization can be prodded to accelerate change, to be inflated, so that malfunctions within it are caused by internal inconsistencies, which lead to gross inefficiencies—behaviorally and mechanically.

The sound organization is managed to accommodate change at a rate required by its external environment, and with a reciprocal degree of stability to attain desired efficiency. Management is responsible for evaluating, designing, and activating the programs required to reach that delicate ratio between change and balance—or dynamic equilibrium. That challenge leads to the need for analytical frameworks. The conceptual overview presented in Figure III.1 is offered as one such model. Let us consider, first, its organic nature, and second, its four major subsets.

Organic Nature

It seems apparent that organizations are organic in nature. Thus, an overview developed to depict sound organizational relationships should show that the organization *requires systematic* coordination of its parts to form an integrated whole.

You will notice in Figure III.1 that the organic makeup of the conceptual overvew includes four major classifications: Environmental consonance, common purpose, social system, internal consistency. Since an organization is dependent on, and emerges from, the broader environment, this is the point at which to break into the system. An analysis of the external environment identifies unfulfilled needs that can be filled by an organization. Common purpose is based on external needs, support, and expectations. External influences provide opportunities and impose constraints. Thus, the vector in Figure III.1 moves from the environment to common purpose. The common purpose, once set, is basic and fundamental. Common purpose anchors all other organizational arrangements. Goals serve, in the short run, as institutionalized imperatives. The

INTERNAL SUBSYSTEMS
(Hierarchy of Plans)

> **TECHNICAL**
> **ECONOMIC**
> **PHYSICAL:**
> > Internal ecology
> > artifacts
>
> **BEHAVIORAL:**
> > roles, norms, values
> > status
> > informal interaction
> > traditions and customs
> > ceremonies, rituals, and symbolism
>
> **MANAGERIAL:**
> > leadership styles
> > work processes
> > authority
> > incentives
> > formal communications
> > control

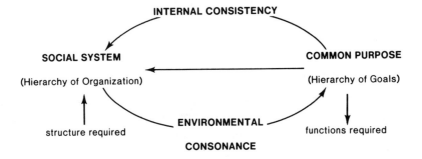

RECEPTIVE TO CHANGE:
> constituent groups
> groups served
> customs and traditions of other
> > units in classification
> > (e.g., industry)
>
> technology
> economy
> values, mores, ethos
> public opinion
> political trends
> legal climate
> markets (labor, capital, land,
> > equipment, materials)

RESPONSIVE TO FORCES URGING CHANGE:
> able
> willing

Figure III.1. Conceptual Overview of an Organization. (Source: *The Nature of Organizations,* Robert Grandford Wright, Dickenson Publishing Co., 1977.)

framework for the social system can then be formed as the first step toward providing the means to aspire to enterprise goals. Thus, the middle vector moves from the common purpose (hierarchy of goals) to the formation of the framework (hierarchy of organization) for a social system. Last, subsystems are developed to tie overall goals back to the people in the formal organizational hierarchy. This step is required so that the people will have support subsystems—behavioral, technical, physical, economic, and managerial—to pursue the goals of the enterprise. Therefore, the last vector points from goals to the people in the social system.

In general, when goals are supported by the broader environment and when formation of the social system and its supportive subsystems are consistent with each other and together serve as the means to reach enterprise goals—we may conclude that a sound organization exists. Contrastingly, if goals are incongruent with external demands, and the formal structure and subsystems are inconsistent with each other and with goals—we may conclude that a weak organization exists.

This, then, is the organic nature of the conceptual overview of an organization, and a preview to its interrelatedness. Now, let us probe more deeply into the composition of the major components in the model. In the four brief discussions of components that follow, we will consider the conditions that cause sound functions and malfunctions in each.

Environmental Consonance

A sound enterprise is *receptive* and *responsive* to changing external forces, and thus ensures its long-run survival. It is dependent upon that environment for support. Those environmental influences presented in **Chapter II** are outlined in the lower part of Figure III.1. The organization's designers maintain a surveillance of those changes that will affect the organization's goals and the means to reach those goals. This is the major interface. The organization develops "sensing" devices so that it can be receptive to those forces urging change. At times, "change" means adapting to external forces; at other times, it means influencing outside forces. Whatever the response, the enterprise is receptive. Beyond the apparent structural influences (e.g., constituent groups, groups served, customs, and traditions, etc.), leaders stay abreast of the subtle cultural nuances (values, mores, ethos) that lead to changing expectations by constituent groups, groups served, and public opinion.

Yet, a receptivity to outside forces alone is inadequate. Leaders of viable organizations also maintain a personal resilience. They also ensure that the bureaucratizing processes necessary for efficiency are adaptable. Finally, they encourage the people in the organization to be culturally and temperamentally able and willing to accept change, *as a requirement of organized life.*

There are serious areas for malfunction here. First, as an organization grows secure, it tends to grow introspective—to become so concerned with internal efficiencies that it becomes oblivious to external constraints and opportunities. Second, specialization causes data to be selectively perceived, often in incomprehensible fragments. Next, some enterprises "hear" data from only certain aspects of their environment, to the neglect of other potentially valuable inputs. As examples, a hospital may "listen" to changing technology and skills, a business to economic information, a school to alumni, a church to laymen—all to the exclusion of other valuable predictors of change. Further, some leaders over time cast in concrete their definition of the operating environment. Hence, they tend to screen out data that does not agree with that definition. Last, organizations can become obsolete if they serve as retreats for those persons determined to preserve sameness. As John W. Gardner put it:

> Men become prisoners of their procedures. . . . There are plenty of old pros who use their skill and experience to block progress rather than advance it. . . . The vast, leaden weight of vested interest is everywhere. . . . Whenever a reorganization is proposed some people object because they have become inseparably attached to old arrangements.[4]

Common Purpose

In the effective organization, common purposes, or goals, are realistic, yet challenging, as they relate to the external environment and internal capabilities. Once goals are formed, key people agree to the overall goals of the enterprise and to their priorities. In turn, the broad objectives are restated throughout the enterprise so that people in all positions know their parts in pursuing top-level goals. Through this process, a hierarchy of goals is formed. The overall purpose of the organization is communicated so that each participant knows not only what is expected of him, but also *why* it is expected; that is, how his contribution fits into overall goals. It is *only* in this way that all members of the organization can identify with the overall mission, and it is only with identification that members can become dedicated to that mission. The ordering of goals infers what functions need to be filled. These functions will, in turn, be reflected in the structure of the organization.

Here, there are a number of ways in which damaging ambiguities can be caused. Goals are often unrealistic. And at times confusion exists among key people as to what is really important; then, adherence to procedures acquires great importance and pursuit of real goals becomes less important. There are frequent cases where the overall goals are not supported by subgoals. Finally, there are instances where subordinate goals are not related to enterprise goals. As a result, subordinates are given the "what, when, how, and where" of their responsibilities, but the all-important "why" is missing. Then leaders echo the familiar refrain, "I don't know why our people are not as involved and dedicated to this work as we were. . . ." Could it be that subordinates feel alienated if directives appear to be arbitrarily imposed because the reasons for the directives are withheld?

Social System

In a sound enterprise, it is apparent that the formal structure of the system reflects the functions required to attain overall goals. Functional-structural logic prevails, anchored in goals. (The relationship is noted in Figure III.1 under Common Purpose and Social System.) Leaders, consequently, can evaluate the congruence of arrangements by relating the hierarchy of goals back to the hierarchy of the organization. You may recall from **Chapter II** that common purpose, stated as a hierarchy of goals, is designed to move from overall, broad objectives down to narrow, specific standards for the lowest participants. Conversely, the social system, acting as a hierarchy of functions, is designed to move from the apex of the top leader downward to the broad diversified array of positions at the lowest level. Therefore, the hierarchy of goals is again shown to be in an inverse relationship to the hierarchy of the organization.

The design of the anatomy of a system has serious pitfalls. Often the organization fails to support goals. At times, people have been placed in positions with insufficient authority to reach or exceed goals. At other times, the organization is ornamented with functional positions having little or nothing to do with the mission of the enterprise. But, most commonly, as goals and functions change, the structure of the organization remains unchanged. Institutionalized "temples" tend to go unchallenged, though their tenets and rituals are outmoded. This is, perhaps, one of the major factors contributing to Gardner's observation that "most organizations have a structure that was designed to solve problems that no longer exist."[5]

Internally Consistent Subsystems

A number of subsystems are required to move the collective efforts of people toward enterprise goals. These internal subsystems are outlined in the upper part of Figure III.1. Their influence prevails in all organizations—a primitive tribe, or a highly sophisticated organization. They are classified as the physical, technical, economic, managerial, and behavioral subsystems of an organization. These subsystems of the organizational system are required to bring order and efficiency to collective human endeavors. In sound enterprises, they are designed to encourage members to participate in achieving enterprise goals, but in a calibrated, patterned, efficient manner. Yet, to do so, each common subsystem complements all other subsystems, and in total, supports the overall goals.

For example, consider an enterprise that has the goal of being a leader in its field of endeavor. Consider further that its structure is designed to geographically decentralize its subunits, and to staff each subunit with research and development people. To stimulate innovation, the organization must design and build appropriate subsystems for support. Values would support creative ideas and change, status would be granted to the research and development people, an avant-garde tradition created, with roles, norms, incentives, authority, control, communications; with the technology and physical artifacts designed so that the means to the goals—leadership in the field—receive backing. Thus, the subsystems are internally consistent with each other and, together, with the goal.

Nearly all organizations, however, have some inconsistencies. Some are fraught with gross, efficiency-draining ambiguities. They arise subtly; they are insidious. A goal is changed, but subsystems remained fixed (say, quality takes priority over quantity, yet incentives remain constant); or, one subsystem is changed, but no adjustment is made in mutually dependent subsystems (perhaps, authority is centralized, but communications, incentives, and control stay the same); or, indeed, an external pressure may cause a change in both the hierarchies of goals and social system, but a reappraisal of integral systems is neglected (thus, all support—economic, physical, technical, behavioral, and managerial—is permitted to malfunction.)

Internal inconsistencies are widespread across organizations. Most, however, are not so chronic that they are debilitating. Indeed, they cause inefficiencies—but rarely do they cause organizational demise. This is probably so because other comparable, if not competing, enterprises also have internal inconsistencies that cause inefficiencies. So, since efficiency is a *relative* measure of success, organizations appear to be comparably efficient—and so they survive. No, inefficiency is not the typical death-blow causing organizations to fail. Inability or unwillingness to adjust to changing (often, rapidly changing) external demands is the typical final blow under which organizations fall—and this point applies equally to all closed and unchanging organizations, be they governments, universities, businesses, marriages, or whatever the organization—no matter its purpose.

Internal inconsistencies simply impede progress, not necessarily block it. The old family car, as a system, gets us where we wish to go, but internal inconsistencies in design and power will cost us considerable time, fuel, and patience. Humans individually and in organized endeavors are vastly resourceful. So they work around the web of ambiguities, and if the ambiguities are not gross, get the job done. However, inefficiencies occur because of voids, redundancies, and unnecessary conflicts. These conditions can in turn cause confusion, frustration, demoralization, alienation, and withdrawal.

The Life Cycle of an Organization[6]

Organizational systems tend to move over a life cycle, or span, somewhat as a human being evolves from infancy to childhood, then to adulthood and old age. An organization typically evolves through four stages—formative stage, mature stage, aging stage, and demise stage.

Let us witness the typical life cycle of a business organization.

Formative Stage

In the beginning an organization is formed by an entrepreneur as the means to attain some goal. During this embryonic period of development, the leadership is concerned mostly with securing inputs, converting them to outputs through a production process (conversion), and then selling the outputs. The reference points of the founder are certain key critical aspects of the external environment, e.g., sources of inputs, markets, and competition.

Internally, there are only a few participants usually highly motivated by the spirit of entrepreneurialship, by the opportunity to do something new and significant, and by the prospect of significantly high financial rewards and status. Everyone interacts with everyone else. Everyone either wins or loses. Systems within emerge in a half-design, half-random way. Procedures, organization, and physical facilities are often makeshift, temporary, and inadequate. Efficiency thus suffers. Yet, an informal, adaptive entrepreneurial spirit prevails.

Mature Stage

Sources of inputs, the conversion process, and a market are somehow secured by the original highly motivated group. With growth, pressures are felt for efficiency. The organization is functionalized as a consequence in this stage. Each functionalized division, such as, engineering, production, marketing, and finance is under the direct control of the key people who originally created the organization. Often, their skills and talents are now supplemented with the addition of various technical specialists. Internal subsystems for work processes, communications, incentives, and control are designed. They include such techniques for efficiency as cost accounting systems, inventory control, purchasing procedures, incentive plans, budgets, work standards, formal communication lines, and permanently added facilities and machines. Authority is still centralized with the original key people.

As the organization matures, further pressures for additional inputs—especially money—make themselves felt. Coincidentally, with growth, upper-managers start to lose day-to-day contact with operative people and problems. They worry about loss of control—even though they are dedicated and work long hours. They are nudged to the final solution of delegating more authority to responsibility centers down the line and thereby to decentralizing the organization.

The leaders recognize and take advantage of the characteristic equifinality of the system they manage. That is, the system can reach its goals in a number of ways. In this instance, either through centralized or decentralized authority arrangements. The day-to-day operative details are delegated to plant and marketing managers so that overall strategies can receive major concentration by top management. Control over subordinate managers is exercised through specified annual goals, such as sales revenues, unit production, and budgets. We should take note here that lower managers are now accountable for inputs, conversion, and output.

Aging Stage

Top management becomes further removed from internal operations in the aging phase. With a satisfactory return on investment by the company, they search for acquisitions of other operations. A number of the original entrepreneurial managers leave the firm in this stage or are shunted aside (or upward) because this stage in the evolutionary path of the company requires more managerial conceptual skills and fewer innovative technical skills than in its earlier stages of development.

Key professional managers now rarely visit the production plants, procedures become more exacting and specific, communications grow even more formalized and flow mostly from the top, activities seem more important than goals, and since managers perceive that they are losing touch, formally exacted controls grow in dominance.

Special efforts are made to coordinate activities and tasks in the aging stage. Often products and brands are grouped in some sort of matrix arrangement; formal planning procedures and reviews (such as, management by objectives) are instituted; numerous central staff people are appointed for control; careful reviews are made of budget and capital expenditures; and a re-centralization is made of certain key technical functions, such as engineering and personnel.

The organization in the aging stage is highly bureaucratized. It has grown to a point where it realizes certain economies of large-scaled operations. Yet, in the process of attaining its present form it is highly likely that it has lost its entrepreneurial spirit.

Demise Stage

The organizational system simply runs down in this stage. It is termed, as you may recall, entropy. The degeneration is caused often by an overemphasis in internal affairs to the neglect of responding to field forces. This is accomplished often by a disproportionate amount of resources being invested in system maintenance rather than productive output. In the opinion of an astute observer:

> The eventual consequence of this phase is rigor mortis—procedure begins to take precedence over problem solving, and red tape makes the organization so stable that it is no longer able to react to change.[7]

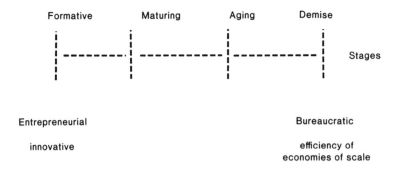

Figure III.2. Balancing Innovation and Efficiency

During the organization's decline, managers emphasize the need for greater flexibility. Real-time information systems are integrated with daily decision making processes; sensitivity training is conducted to bring people (back) together; team action is adopted for problem identification and solution; and fewer specialists are retained at headquarters.

The entire effort here is implemented to regain the more free-wheeling, highly motivated attributes of the entrepreneurial spirit that was present in the formative stage, but now combined with efficiencies and economies of scale of the large, complex organizational system. Viewed diagrammatically in Figure III.2, managers are attempting to move the organization back along the continuum to become more entrepreneurial and less bureaucratic. The objective is to move the capabilities of the organization to a point near the maturing stage where processes are bureaucratized to a sufficient degree to yield efficiency, but the firm is also able to respond innovatively to necessary change. This is the artful application of organizational design to achieve appropriate degrees of "dynamic equilibrium."

For another view of the life cycle of an organization, we invite you to analyze the case of "The Islanders" in **Appendix III.A.** The dramatization reveals a more detailed presentation of what goes on in each stage, and illustrates the effect on participants of internal inconsistencies and rigidities. To gain a full share of enrichment from this case, picture the members of your group—with you included, of course—as the members of the ill-begotten islanders. The organizational adventure that unfolds could have happened in a variety of types of organizational endeavors—to an institute to help blind children, to an aborted space colony, or to a production system's planning department.

Summary

An organizational system differs from a group of people in significant ways. Organizations are designed to reach organizational goals, to provide inducements to members to ensure commitment, and to impose sufficient structure. Once created, organizations—as open systems—have needs.

Viewed at arm's length, an organization can be seen as a conceptual overview with organic segments dealing with common purpose (functions), social system (structure), internal consistency (subsystems), and environmental consonance (system's field forces). A state of changing balance—essential to organizational survival—exists when these organic segments are designed and managed in a calibrated way.

An organization historically tends to move through a life cycle, from a formative stage, to a mature stage, to an aging stage, and finally, to a demise stage. The metamorphic path is not an absolute predestiny, but rather a tendency caused by rational responses by leaders to conditions at varied stages over the life span of the organization. Managers, as organizational systems designers, attempt to design the enterprise so that it can realize both economies of scale (efficiency) and entrepreneurial innovation (effectiveness). Thus, by careful design the organizational system can thrive with a realistic balance of dynamic equilibrium.

Notes

1. Robert Grandford Wright, *The Nature of Organizations,* (Rancho Palos Verdes, California: Paradigm Publishing Company, 1983), p. 156.
2. Robert Grandford Wright, *Exploring Vital Elements of Organization and Management,* (Dubuque, Iowa: Kendall/Hunt, 1978), pp. 93–103.
3. Chester I. Barnard, *The Functions of the Executive,* (Cambridge, Massachusetts: Harvard University Press, 1938), p. 73.
4. John W. Gardner, *No Easy Victories,* (New York: Harper and Row Publishers, 1968), pp. 44–45.
5. *Ibid.*
6. This presentation is based on the observations of Dr. T. F. Gautschi, "The Life Cycle of an Organization," Design Management Forum, *Design News,* April 8, 1974, pp. 147–148.
7. *Ibid,* p. 148.

Appendix III-A

Life Cycle of an Organization*

The whole that counts in building a system or in measuring its performance is an increasingly larger whole, one that does not stop even at its own boundaries but extends into the environment to which it relates.

John A. Beckett[1]

It is apparent that when one's endeavors exceed one's individual capacity in either size or complexity, it is wise to merge efforts with those of other persons. When joint activities of the individuals are structured and coordinated toward common goals, an organization forms. As indicated earlier, an organization changes as a result of changing goals, means to goals, environmental demands, and roles or role relationships of its participants. Pressures for change are perpetual. Though certain enterprises have managed to maintain a dynamic equilibrium—moving balances over time—most have been unable to do so. Some have failed to survive because they would not or could not change; others, because they could not maintain the degree of efficiency expected so that more efficient organizations filled the void.

In **Chapter III**, we saw that organizations have functional needs required for survival, and that these needs stem from goals based on conditions in their environment. We found that organizations are born out of social necessity. Further, we learned earlier that although they are initially justified by social and economic needs, organizations are expected to use efficiently scarce resources—people, money, land, equipment, and/or raw materials—and to effectively adapt to the changing needs and expectations of support groups. To do so, the conceptual model of sound organization behavior shown in figure III.A.1 was introduced and discussed. Filling the conditions of this model, though important for all types of organizations, becomes critical for those that compete with other enterprises for survival.

---

*Source: *The Nature of Organizations,* Chapter 4.

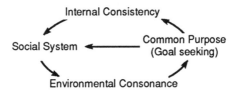

Figure III.A.1. Conceptual Model of a Sound Organization

We can now advance, in this chapter, to observe the behavior of a "living" organization and analyze that behavior as it relates to the conceptual model. From this account, the reader can gain an insight into the reasons organizations are strong or weak, efficient or inefficient, viable or rigid. A fictional case will be used to illustrate the forming, maturing, aging, and declining phases in an organization's life cycle.

Introduction to the Islander Case

Consider now an organization born out of functional necessity. It was designed to serve its purpose efficiently and effectively. Then the enterprise lost its ability to perform under newly imposed demands and finally dissolved. To take an organization through the complete life cycle, in a suitably brief discussion, it is necessary to assume a bizarre event. The situation was selected so that the demands on the entity could be changed abruptly and rapidly. The simplified fictional account that follows was chosen not for its eccentricities, but rather because its striking contrasts illustrate what can happen to an organization over its life cycle.

The Islanders: An Illustration

Picture a group of thirty to forty people enjoying a cruise on a pleasure yacht in the Caribbean Sea. Imagine further that the voyagers are taking part in certain popular shipboard activities such as fishing, swimming, shuffleboard, and card-playing. At this point, they enjoy casual, quickly changing social relationships arising from informal arrangements and a mutual desire for pleasure. Since pleasure can be achieved individually, in pairs, or in larger informal groups, no organization is needed.

Genesis of an Organization

Far out to sea, an unpredicted storm suddenly closes in on the yacht restricting visibility and making it impossible to navigate. As the boat pitches and yaws out of control, the hull strikes a floating object that severs the bow and makes evacuation mandatory. Passengers and crew man the lifeboats, setting their course for a land mass seen mistily on the distant horizon. In time, the castaways beach their boats and take stock of their situation. Though the lifeboats are sadly damaged, the people are at the moment safe from harm. But immediately two critical questions arise: First, is there enough food and water to support them? And second, are they invading a territory defended by hostile inhabitants?

Confronted with these threatening specters, mature people feel strongly the urge for self-preservation. They recognize the limitations of any single person in trying to conquer such obstacles. A reasoning adult (unlike the children who retrogressed to a primitive existence in *The Lord of the Flies*) becomes acutely aware of individual limitations on strength, endurance, and the diversity of skills required for survival. The people band together. Each sees strength in numbers and actively supports organized effort. Under the circumstances, it would be senseless for any person or group of people to try to dissociate themselves from the larger band and fend for themselves. It would be more reasonable to expect that the overall group would block attempts to fragment it, attempts that would sap the enterprise of its strength.

But can even a cohesive group fulfill the basic needs of its members? Probably not, at least not at a level of efficiency required by this situation. Efficient human effort comes when a group is structured so that its activities are patterned in such a way that they lead directly to goals. Stated differently, counterproductive effort that impedes goal attainment is minimized.

Leadership

First, the *group* needs a central authority to give it overall guidance, to allocate resources, and to keep its members headed toward the same goals. In a word, leadership is needed. It is required by functional necessity. Assume now that the members of the shipwrecked party assemble to choose a leader. Would it necessarily be one who acted as an informal leader in arranging social events aboard ship? Would it automatically be a ship's officer who had demonstrated ability as a seafaring leader? Or would it be a member of the group who was reputed to be an effective manager of a commercial enterprise at home? Perhaps any one of these persons would be candidates for the position of authority. However, none may have the background and attributes essential for leadership *in this particular situation:* a situation in which survival is possible, but only by using extreme measures.

Consider the appropriate traits of a candidate for a position of authority and responsibility here. It might be valuable to the group if the person had experience in leading others safely through trials brought on by a similar threatening situation. Under the dangers that seem to prevail, a candidate should probably possess the technical skills required to provide the group with food, shelter, and security. Stamina, strength, and authoritative bearing to command may be necessary to a group under stress. Further, the person may need to be decisive, mentally alert, an incisive communicator, and able to marshall group efforts. In sum, the characteristics of the situation suggest certain requirements of leadership:

Leadership Traits
Experience as a specialist in field (military or other)
Technical skills
Strength and stamina
Authoritative manner
Decisiveness
Mental adroitness
Ability to communicate incisively
Ability to organize

If leadership is to get results from people, it must be situationally appropriate—or contingent on operating requirements.

Authority

Second, the leader must gain and use authority to accomplish the required tasks. What is the source of this authority or influence? Authority generally comes from a formal source. These are usually private property (entrepreneurial), public property (governmental), spiritual needs (religious), or public decree (legal). Yet no institution now exists;

there is only a group of people. Authority must originate with the group members. Each must agree to give up certain aspects of free will to the leader so that the total group may benefit. Such awarding of authority is akin to public decree, or consent, but without the institutional arrangements. In the place of an institution dispensing authority, it is generated by the people based upon their needs. It is often called the "authority of the situation." Rather than coming down from the top, it is acquired from each subordinate member and delegated upward.

Each member has effectively relinquished part of his or her self-determination to make possible group determination through an organization set up to reach goals. Each member also expects to reap the rewards of the affiliation: physical well-being, security, order, perhaps even social and psychological gratification. But is subjection to power worth it? Though authority is power over others, the idea of power is not at issue. Power has been legitimized, or at least rationalized to be perceived as "accepted authority." The negative feeling associated with power over free men has been transformed to "rightful power," that is, authority granted by the group because of the unusual situation. Often, rather elaborate symbols and complex rituals are projected upon those in power by those governed in order to provide an aura of legitimacy. In these ways power is converted to acceptable authority.

In any event, persons join the common effort because to them the rewards outweigh the sacrifices. Authority is accepted because leadership is required to fulfill the needs of the group.

Formal Structure

Third, the leader (with the followers' support) identifies the *major goal* of the group. The common purpose is survival. The *subgoals* required to reach the overall goal are providing food, shelter, and protection against attack. Subgoals are needed to further delineate what lesser objectives must be achieved to reach the overriding mission, or common purpose.

With the goal and subgoals defined, the leader can now move to the fourth step, that of providing for the fulfillment of *functions* required by *organizing* the people within the group so that the subgoals and in turn, the overall goal, are met quickly. With subgoals of providing food, shelter, and protection from portent attack, the functions would logically include securing food (gathering, hunting, seining, or whatever else is feasible), building (providing materials, trimming, framing, siding, thatching, and so on), and providing security (lookouts, listening posts, patrols, or other). When functions have been determined, they must be reflected in the organization, if they are to be accomplished. Functions are activities required to attain goals. They are the logical bases for organizing people.

Organizing deals with assigning members to one of the three major areas of activities so that each one can make the greatest contribution to the overall effort. This is a *division of labor* to bring about *specialization*. The organizing technique is based on the idea that individuals have unique backgrounds of experience, skills, and physical traits that make them better suited for one task than another. Further, the repeated performance of that task in cooperation with those doing related jobs will result in efficiencies beyond those that could be reasonably expected from a generalist—a "jack of all trades" working with first one work group and later another.

The leader would doubtless allocate the tasks to the individuals best suited to pursue each activity. For example, those with backgrounds and skills in hunting, fishing, or scouting might be assigned to gather food, those experienced in carpentry, to build shelters; and those with military or police training, to provide security from attack. *Departments of functional activities* would thus be formed. Since the activities would take place in different technical areas and places, the leader of the group would doubtless appoint leaders for each subgroup. At this stage in the life cycle of the organization, superior technical abilities would probably be the determining factor in the selection of each of the three intermediate leaders, that is, those functioning between the workers and the top leader.

In turn, the intermediate leaders would sort out the activities required within each major department. They would then assign subtasks to members within their respective work units. For instance, in the unit constructing shelter, several members would be assigned to gather raw materials for building, others to prepare the materials for use, others to build framing, while others would specialize in applying siding and thatching roofs. These finer degrees of specialization can bring about further efficiencies as long as the common purpose, and each member's part in its attainment, is clearly understood.

The basic framework that shows the way an organization should function has been formed. It is called the *formal organization*. It limits, and sets guidelines for, the relationships of those within the social system.

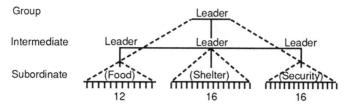

Figure III.A.2. Genetic Organization

It delimits areas of activities. It defines authority and communication flows and identifies points of responsibility. It suggests role behavior and appropriate role relationships with those within and outside each functional work unit. Such a framework quite simply acts as an outside governor on human behavior, defining the boundaries between activities and providing structure. The structure, based upon functions, serves as the primary means by which the enterprise can begin to pursue its goals. A formal organization chart can simplify (unfortunately, also oversimplify) human interaction by providing a graphic illustration of the basic framework. The charting of the newly formed or genetic, formal arrangements by the castaways would be as shown in Figure III.A.2.

A plan for the organization of the group now exists. An unbroken line links the individual at the top of the structure to the subordinate lowest in the hierarchy. This provides the means for authority and communications to flow in a patterned way. Each of the three levels, or scales, in the hierarchy indicates an authority level that is the same horizontally across the chart. And each leader has clearly defined areas of accountability and authority. These are termed *spans of management,* or in the military, *spans of command.* They are identified by the broken lines on the chart. One can see that the span of management for the group leader in charge of food is twelve subordinates, while the group leaders accountable for shelter and security each supervises sixteen.

Delegation

At this point in the life cycle of the organization, a structure has been provided. The static framework of what will become an organization exists, and a group has been mechanically divided and arranged. But no organization exists because an organization is characterized by orderly activities, events, and movement among people—in other words, a dynamic social system.

The catalyst that brings about action is the delegation of authority. In the example used, the group leader delegates authority to the intermediate leaders to perform the duties or tasks assigned to them. The overall leader then holds them accountable to him for results. In turn, the intermediate leaders delegate authority to their subordinates to perform their respective tasks. They must then hold their subordinates accountable for the successful completion of these tasks.

With the formal organization serving as a structure to provide order to human endeavor, the delegation of authority triggers a chain reaction of decisions, actions, and obligations; a dynamic patterning of events or happenings commences to convert the original rigidly structured group into a social system. An organization is born.

Sources of Inefficiency

In the beginning, the command to produce food, shelter, and protection brings on a flurry of activities in the various departments accountable for these major tasks. Each member tries to perform the duties as he or she understands them. Some members in the section constructing shelter, for example, locate, secure, and prepare raw materials for construction, while others among them attempt to build frames or coverings. The varied activities, however, lack coordination. Raw materials of one sort or another pile up too high while others are unavailable; framing lags behind necessary covering; and the preparation of one material for use in construction is of poor quality, whereas another of an unnecessarily high quality is produced.

Coincidentally, confusion may arise as to the interrelationships among the intermediate leaders. They may in good faith vie against one another for the use of certain resources to fulfill the responsibilities of their respective areas of activity as they understand them. For instance, the security leader may be using building materials for, say, a vital lookout tower—materials that are then not available to the shelter leader, who also needs them. So, tradeoffs become necessary.

And finally, at the outset, the top leader may be uncertain about his role or role relationship to subordinate leaders. Confusion may exist over the best means to achieve the overall purpose of the organization. The leader may be unsure about the proper allocation of human resources to serve as means to reach the goals. This person may be taking tentative action and making interim decisions with a high degree of uncertainty.

The Emerging Organization

The organization has now been launched. Beset by pressures of unknown food sources and the possible presence of hostile inhabitants, this social structure would be formed and activated quickly after the party's landing on shore. It has a common purpose (goals) clearly understood by its participants. It is highly sensitive to external conditions and able to react quickly to changes. The organization is basically internally consistent in its use of authority, communications, and rewards. The social system, however, is somewhat inefficient because it lacks coordination of efforts at all levels. This is caused by no chronic ailment; it occurs because the participants have not been interacting long enough to develop common sets of roles, norms, and values. These are needed so that acceptable individual and interpersonal behavior can be molded. Each member needs to know what others expect and what, in turn, can be expected of others. In an organization, in contrast to more casual social groups, there is heavier reliance upon formally prescribed rules defining acceptable behavior.

Maturing of an Organization

When an organization is first formed, its basic framework comes from structural-functional dependencies. For instance, in our shipwreck example, it was found that to achieve the ultimate objective (survival), certain basic needs (food, shelter, and security) had to be filled. In turn, the design of the structure of the organization was dependent upon how these tasks could best be accomplished. The ultimate objective (common purpose) required subgoals, which effectively identified functional areas of specialization needed within the social system. Expressed graphically, the sequential reasoning process for organizing looks like Figure III.A.3.

Life Cycle of an Organization

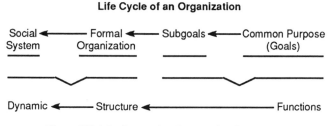

Figure III.A.3. Reasoning Process for Organizing

Once structurally organized, the delegation of authority from the leaders brought about human interaction to generate cooperative effort. The simple production structure formed was sufficient to meet task demands. A primitive organization had emerged.

Coordination

Though goal-directed activities soon began, we found that the level of output by individual participants was unpredictable and uncoordinated. As a result, the organization was relatively inefficient when seen in light of its productive potential. A leader, uninitiated in organizational behavior, might assume too quickly that a redistribution of tasks is immediately needed to bring on desired performance. Probably reformation will be required, since the organization was originally designed with only a rough idea of the amount of work needed from each of the varied units. Reshaping of formal arrangements—a reorganization—should not be done, however, until the members have had a chance to perform acceptably and to merge their achievements with others.

Design of Formal Patterns

Acceptable behavior in organizations relies heavily on formal rules. The development of acceptable (as opposed to unacceptable) behavior is influenced by values commonly shared by the participants and gained from prior experiences within and outside the organization. More germane to the success of the total organization, however, is the need for the leaders to orient members to the norms necessary for the endeavor's survival. Formal patterns of conduct *that are largely predictable* flow from the participants' understanding of a system's norms, roles, and values.

Leaders in any enterprise establish formal patterns to guide behavior because they are the bases for the integration of organized social endeavors. *Norms* are the expectations shared by members in the organizing of performance. They are demands for the minimum results sought from by all system members, though the term *norm* may seem to imply average performance. To achieve the norms, *roles* are used to define expected forms of behavior appropriate to completing tasks assigned. Regardless of personal whims, roles are required of all members so that each plays a part based upon his or her functional relationships to others in the pursuit of goals. The interrelatedness of roles and inter-dependent sets of activities add cohesion to an organization. One member's goals act as another's means to reach different goals. Thus, well-defined and broadly understood roles enable all members to see their specific contributions in functional relationship with those of their fellow members. And finally, *values* are views shared by the members of the organization concerning the acceptance or rejection of system goals, subgoals, norms, and roles. Shared values, as they apply to individual participation, cause the individual to adopt organizational goals with varying degrees of commitment. They influence the degree of acceptance, support, and dedication propelling an organized effort.

Norms set minimum levels of acceptable performance; values act as appeals for performance superior or inferior to minimal expectations. As an example, norms establish standards of output expected from one of our castaways assigned to gather food. They also set the limits beyond which there will be penalties for not attaining the goals. But if the idea of securing food is viewed by the gatherer as a contribution to the security and survival of the organization, it would be the consequence of an appeal to values above the norms. Stated another way, acceptance of the task based on values would come from an understanding of the importance of superior performance by the individual to the welfare of all the people in the organization.

In sum, norms, roles, and values can bring on specialization of task efforts, provide the means for integration and continuity, give rise to the standards for individual conduct and performance. When participants understand clearly the demands imposed by these influences, they serve as means of control, that is, they reduce inappropriate behavior. Thus, acceptable behavior is ensured because it supports the functional requirements needed to reach organizational goals.

Rules

Now let's return to the hypothetical example of the organization formed to serve the shipwrecked castaways. Assume that the leadership at this time recognizes the need for standards to establish acceptable behavior patterns. At the second, or maturing, stage of the organization, leaders formulate and begin to enforce rules to govern behavior.

For example, you may recall that one problem appeared in the unit formed to build shelters. Coordination was lost because unusually high stocks of one type of raw material tended to be built up while other types of supplies were depleted. Therefore, construction lacked continuity and lost efficiency. This imbalance was the result of unacceptable behavior on the part of members. They did not understand what constituted acceptable behavior. Assume that the leader and workers in this activity soon find the best flows of materials for a balanced supply and develop shared expectations of performance to meet the requirement. The leader then can coordinate the activities to maintain a daily flow of a certain mix of materials, and to disperse it to given areas so that it can be processed for use in building. Each member is assigned a part in the overall task. Once the assignments are accepted, the members are provided with role requirements. Further, the leader encourages the gatherers to perceive the goal as their own. Once a mutuality of goals exist, norms are established. And finally, if the material gatherers sense the urgent need for shelter and throw themselves into dedicated effort that creates a stock far beyond that required for a single day, their behavior would be in response to values.

During the maturing stage, leaders and followers attempt to eliminate inconsistencies caused by confused role behavior and role relationships. This is done by formulating and enforcing rules, which then generate a higher intensity of authority. And this becomes the basis of the continuing use of authority for the self-maintenance and productivity of an organization.

Transformation

Following the establishment of rules, we can expect changes in role behavior. The effects of these changes in behavioral patterns as they influence production will then be felt and a reanalysis of formal organizational arrangements can take place. This is required to ensure the proper use of resources, the desired degree of specialization, the coordination of tasks within and among work units, and the desirable span of management. Once done, internal inconsistencies will have been removed or minimized. The organization has been moved into a stage of maturity in its life cycle.

Consider now the capabilities of this healthy, mature organization. The reader will recall that two major external forces impinge on the stranded voyager's organization: (1) uncertainty as to adequate amounts of food, and (2) uncertainty as to the presence of hostile inhabitants. To

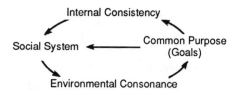

Figure III.A.4. Conceptual Mode of an Efficient and Effective Organization

analyze the status of this organization, it would be helpful to reintroduce the conceptual model of an efficient, effective formal organization originally presented in Chapter III (see Figure III.A.4).

Now, let us evaluate this organization as to its ability to achieve both productivity and self-maintenance. To make the analysis, we need answers to such questions as: Is the common purpose of the organization, including the relation of subgoals to the overall undertaking, clear to its participants? Is it sensitive to environmental forces and adaptable to them? Is it internally consistent, that is, do the internal systems of activity support each other and provide the means to goal attainment? Is the social system cohesive, or is the system's self-maintenance threatened by potential fragmentation of members? Does it produce, thereby fulfilling its social function? Each of these questions will be examined in the following subsections.

Common Purpose. The anchor to which any social system is tied is common purpose. In this instance, the threatening aspects of the environment (hunger, thirst, attack, even inclement weather) rivet the attention of members of the organization to the basic object (survival) of their mutual endeavors. Further, with such an uncommon, fundamental goal, it is also clear to members that the subgoals are part and parcel of the ultimate goal. Hence, they clearly understand and unanimously endorse both the ends and the means of their venture. Should a member do otherwise, informal groups would probably nudge the dissident back into line.

In addition, the participants can, at this point in the development of the organization, see progress being made through their joint efforts. Activities are set up and executed to provide the basic necessities for life. The payoff is clearly demonstrated to the individuals supporting the organized effort to achieve these goals, or common purposes.

Consonance with External Environment. A social system must maintain a consonance, or compatability, with its environment to survive.

To sustain this harmony between the organization and its particular setting, it must be both sensitive to external changes and able to adjust to new demands as they occur. Thus, an analysis of an organization's capabilities to maintain congruence between its activities and the demands from external forces should be conducted in two parts.

First, we must estimate the degree of its sensitivity to environmental forces. This does not include all environmental forces, of course, but only those to which the system must react. In the organization we have been following, such forces would include changes in food supply, weather, or signs of other threats. Again, fear of physical harm is a potent force in ensuring a perceptive organization. Among the castaways there are not only specially formed units to provide security, food, and shelter, but each person has also appointed him or herself to be a lookout for threats to survival or opportunities to increase security. This means that the objectives of the formal organization are also the goals of the informal groups. This condition, where formal and informal arrangements support each other, provides considerable organizational strength.

Second, if an organization is to be consonant with its external environment, it is necessary to estimate its ability to change. Though mature in one sense, the organization at hand is young in another. It has no rich culture or rituals, no tradition. Its members have not as yet acquired deeply set ways of acting and reacting. Nor is its leadership so confident of its methods of proceeding that it will not change. At this time and under these circumstances, it is easy to introduce modifications.

The seeds for inflexible relationships, however, have been sown. The mere acts of giving unequal shares of authority, of placing members into specific units of activities, and of insisting upon certain role behavior and role relationships will foster resistance to change. Structuring is mandatory for order, but order begets lethargy.

Internal Consistency. Now we come to the subsystems of the organization. We must analyze these aspects to see if they support each other and the overall purpose. We must also find out if they are perceived as serving a rational purpose by the participants subjected to them. For this part of the evaluation, it is well to analyze the array of subsystems undergirding the island organization. Table III.A.1 shows certain classes of internal subsystems, the reasons for their design, and, in addition, their impact upon the members as they might view it.

Internal consistency is attained when the subsystems of activities can be justified as means leading directly to an organization's goals. This condition of inner balance, or homogeneity, is strengthened when the

70

TABLE III.A.1.
Designing Internally Consistent Subsystems

Design of Internal Systems	Organizational Rationale	Participants' Perception of Rationale
Common purpose of survival	Threat	Threat
Subgoals of shelter, food, and security	Basic biological needs and protection of members; fulfill common purpose	Basic individual needs
Autocratic leadership	Fast reaction of total forces	Fast marshalling of members for individual protection
Formal groupings by major tasks	Functionally related to needs of organization	Logical means to provide basic needs of individuals
Direct delegative processes downward	Speed and simplicity	Efficient use of authority
Downward communications	Fast total reaction; little need for upward flow	Fast mobilization to quell attack; little need for upward flow because "experts" are in sensitive positions
Command and control basic to leadership	Cohesion, unity of direction urgently needed	Protection and self-support enhanced by safety in numbers with common cause
Rigorous control of participants' roles	Organizational well-being dependent on individual efforts	Must "pull together" to survive; self-control and informal control appropriate values
Clearly communicated incentives	Individuals share in protection and well-being brought on by organized efforts	Increased chances for survival if broader organization survives. "For my contribution, it provides protection."

participants accept as justifiable arrangements related to organizational needs and goals. Once they accept the rationale for the design of institutional subsystems, members can shoulder the demands placed upon them by such arrangements and direct their attention to their respective tasks. In the absence of a high degree of acceptance, participants spend much of their time and energies trying to change arrangements to meet expectations or to undermine areas that they see as inappropriate.

The mature organization of the islanders is internally consistent. The subsystems are justified as means to goals, both from an organizational and a participant standpoint. Now let us see if the internal systems support each other. Note that all arrangements are designed to facilitate quick, unified reaction to threat. The social system is command-oriented, in response to the demands of the situation. Regimented control is crucial to the venture's success, so leadership is militantly autocratic, delegation and communications unilaterally aimed downward. Authority relationships are clearly drawn to avoid confusion; functionally based formal groupings are charted on simple lines; and appropriate incentives produce contributions to the continuity, cohesiveness, and manageability of the total system. No internal inconsistency can be found here. The orientation of the organization continues to be toward emergency action.

Consider, finally, the effect of the introduction of an inconsistently designed subsystem. Assume that all internal systems are designed for command and control, with the exception, say, of incentives. Consider the effect on behavior of an incentive system geared to reward participants on the basis of their nonconformity and self-determination. The results would be ludicrous—even fatal. Such a basis for rewards would weaken cohesiveness, control, and the ability of the total system to react rapidly and uniformly. Indeed, this internal inconsistency could weaken, if not abort, actions to achieve the common purpose of the organization.

In a relatively simple organization with a clear-cut mission, such as the organization of islanders, there is little chance for major discontinuities to impede progress. It is in more complex social systems with less clearly definable objectives, that inconsistencies of major consequence can arise.

We see, then, that the maturing organization is coordinated both internally and externally to reach its goals. It is thus efficient in the use of its resources and, by maintaining a consonance with its environment, is enabled to achieve long-run effectiveness.

An organization, however, is often subjected to a metamorphosis— that is, a change in form, structure, or substance—after reaching full maturity. The transformation usually is caused by changes or perceived changes in the external environment. In response, the structure is reformed. Assuming it has developed a sound method of operation during its maturing process, there is little justification for its leader or other participants to change their behavior in any substantive way. Perhaps this is the reason leaders of mature organizations often react to issues rather than acting to anticipate change.

Changing Environment

Let us now imagine a major change in the situation of the islanders. Assume that the threat of physical danger is removed. Then the purpose, functions, structure, types of activities, and composition of the total system must in turn be changed.

After organizing, the leaders doubtless would initiate efforts to find out more about the threats imposed by shortages of food or possible attacks by hostile inhabitants. To do so, the top leader would direct an intermediate leader, the head of security, to reconnoiter the unknown areas of the island and report any information obtained. In response, patrols would advance around the island in a pincers movement and return through the midlands. On completing the mission, they arrive back at the base camp and report that no other persons or threatening animals inhabit the island. Further, on the other side of a nearby hill lies a valley holding a meadow rich with abundant game and edible plants and drained by a natural spring providing an apparently inexhaustible source of water. At that instant, threat has been lifted from the group—threat that had provided a common purpose. What happens?

The organization's mission now changes. Its functions are transformed. Its structure must be re-formed to serve as a means to new goals, and its systems reevaluated to achieve the new objectives. The way in which its activities are performed will now change. Its patterns of leadership must be adjusted. In fact, the very nature of the total system will change. Let us look closely at the extent of these changes and their influence on organizational health, that is, efficiency and effectiveness.

Goals

The purpose of the organization changes. It was originally formed for its participants' survival. Now, it must provide the necessities of a small social order, and improved standard of living, and the means for rescue or escape. Though worthy objectives, they are not the sharply defined goal of survival, nor will these new goals inspire total agreement on the best way to reach them.

Functions

The functions of the organization must change since they are directly connected to its new goals. In general, there are two classes of functions to fulfill. The first, for which the organization was originally formed, is closely tied to the physical needs of the people. Yet these needs no longer have their initial urgency. The second function is to provide the institutional means to maintain the organization as a social system and, by doing so, to prevent forces of individual self-interest from destroying it. The organization must provide food, shelter, and protection. But, in addition, it must institutionalize levels of accepted behavior to harness the individual to community action. All of these functions must be fulfilled through means acceptable to the organization's participants under the now-less-urgent situation. In a word, a society must be created.

Structure

The structure of the organization must be re-formed to provide the means to achieve the new functional requirements. Under the newly relaxed environment (the only uncertainties being the time of rescue or the feasibility of escape), the members will need institutionalized means to develop fairly complete societal arrangements. Beyond providing for biological wants, the organization must now act to satisfy needs for such things as law and order, cultural events, spiritual guidance, and governance. In response, the organization necessarily would be dramatically reshaped from its initial form to fill a number of expected, though more nebulous, functions—in contrast to those that it filled originally. It undergoes a change in form called a metamorphosis. A transformation occurs, not unlike a major change in a physical organism, where it would be referred to as metamorphic. It would change from the simple genetic organization to the complex metamorphic organization depicted in Figure III.A.5.

The organization chart, though only a crude estimate of the real changes, illustrates the intricacy of the evolving system required to meet complex functional needs. Note that though the same people are involved, when the organization is fragmented to accommodate new activities, an additional level of leadership is needed. Further, observe that with increasing complexity and the need to provide government, specialized staff advisors are needed. These staff units counsel the leader of the organization and, through this individual, assist the leaders of various functional activities. This is commonly required because line leaders are generalists who often need specialized assistance in a certain area. In sum, increasing functional needs lead to more specialized activities. Then, the activities bring on more organizational arrangements, multiple authority levels, line and staff units, and multiple authority flows.

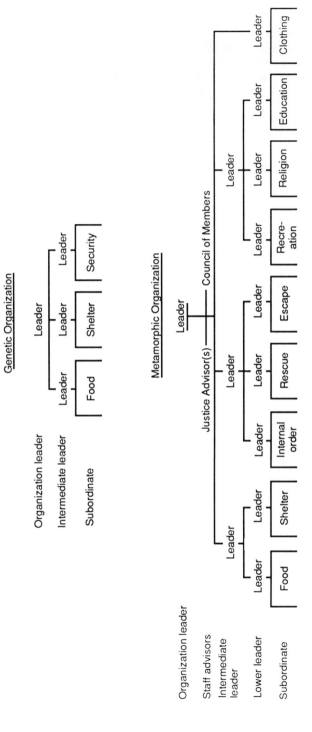

Figure III.A.5. Genetic Organization and Metamorphic Organization

Subsystems

As structural arrangements become more complex, the systems for such elements as authority, delegation, communications, incentives, and control become more difficult to design and manage. This is particularly true if common purpose is lost due to differing interpretations by various members of the group. In the beginning, for instance, authoritative power was used and accepted to make sure that at least enough food was obtained daily to sustain life. Now new expectations have doubtless developed concerning not only the quantity but also the quality and palatability of foods. What combinations of subsystems promise meeting such minimum standards for eating? Can they be merely ordered in the same way minimum quantities of food were? No, the use of authority alone fails to produce high performance when the primary requisite is quality. Perhaps through the use of minimized authority and control, along with maximized incentives and participation by the culinary staff, a high level of cuisine can be produced—assuming, of course, that general agreement can be reached as to what constitutes a "high level of cuisine."

Tempo

With a marked change in environment, the pace at which members perform the activities required by the organization shifts down from intense to relaxed. This adjustment is understandable, since the new organizational setting now permits security, if not comfort. Not only is the rate of interaction slowed, but there is also an accompanying relaxing in the degree of integration. That is, as the demands on the organization grow less intense and its activities more diffuse, the tempo of interaction among members slackens. Thus, the integrating bonds are weakened.

Leadership

The role behavior of leadership changes both in intent and in content when the setting of an organization is altered. The *intent of leadership* here means its determination to act in a certain way toward subordinate members. The *content of leadership* refers to the composition of the leaders' responsibilities to the organization.

Reflect back to the behavioral traits and skills of the leader needed during the beginning of the survivors' organization. Recall that a person was chosen to act as an authoritative, strong commander who could decisively direct, organize, and control people under conditions of stress. This was the *intent of leadership.* Recall further that the situation required that the head be technically competent to provide bodily protection and security for the members. As a result, one with demonstrated abilities to command under adverse conditions, such as a former military leader, might have been selected. This technical ability was required for the *content of leadership.*

Now the organization has moved to a point where the people or the organization no longer need such a vibrant figure to lead, either in intent or content. Consider once again the leadership behavior and skills desired; then evaluate the attributes to be sought in the person who should now lead. The type of leader needed in the new situation must be able to cultivate the individual talents of the members to develop societal arrangements through which standards of living can be improved, commonly held values maintained, and escape or rescue made possible. The behavior and skills required to accomplish these would be quite different from those necessary to lead the organization under its original charter. To fill the leadership role posed by the respective situations, one would normally be expected to possess the following attributes:

Attributes of Leadership in Original Situation	*Attributes of Leadership in Current Situation*
Experience as a specialist in field (military or other)	Experience as a generalist (perhaps in government)
Projecting image of strength	Projecting image of stability
Authoritative in manner	Judicial in manner
Decisive	Deliberative
Mentally adroit	Mentally thoughtful, an arbitrator
An incisive communicator	An emphatic communicator
An organizer	A planner

Though these are merely an estimate, the differences seem necessary under the new situation. They seem more realistic for the leader who must assume the new role—a role shaped by the intent of leadership and the general membership to establish a small society.

The content of leadership must also change with the major organizational change. Leaders are expected to have competency in three major areas: technical, human, and conceptual. Technical skills are essential in mechanical or technological matters; human skills are used in interpersonal relationships; and conceptual skills are needed to solve problems requiring broadened perspective.

The original organization needed someone with specific skills and experience to guide it. Now the situation calls for a person with greater competence in the areas of human and conceptual skills to cope with the broadened fields of activity. Now members expect a less autocratic posture from their leader.

Leadership is effective when it is appropriate to the situation. And situations do change. Some leaders are psychologically prepared to vary their approaches with changing circumstances and are open to learning new skills. If organizations are to be adaptive and flexible systems, leaders must display adaptive and flexible behavioral patterns.

Some leaders, however, (as well as other people) become structured and rigid. They assume a certain approach to people and close out alternative approaches, even as the world changes around them. When unbending, structured individual behavior is confronted by forceful system changes, the system's structure cracks—or structured people are removed.

Assume for our purposes that the leader of the islanders is unable or unwilling to change behavior. So, replacement is required. A change in leaders presupposes that the members of the organization can remove the autocrat and install a new leader with capabilities suitable to the new needs of the organization. Often, however, dictatorial rule persists beyond the time when the organizational situation requires it, as do obsolete subsystems and procedures. It is not uncommon for a dictator to rise to power when an organization (or country) is in trouble and, by insulating the administration against reform, continue to rule beyond the critical stage of the endeavor's development, thereby preserving political power. Though examples of this sort of political self-perpetuation are widespread, it is more useful here to assume that a change in leadership will be made. It is also more realistic when one considers the speed with which the organization of marooned voyagers has been formed and re-formed. It seems doubtful that in such a short time span, leaders could have shielded their positions of authority from a pronounced need for change.

Total System

The final major change will make itself felt on the organization as a whole. And its impact can neither be clearly seen nor accurately understood by simply summing up the changes that have transpired to this point. A social system is greater than the sum of its parts. The impact of change races through it in such a way that the new organization typically develops a quality that is very different from that of the original structure. It is somewhat like a sweeping change of personality in a person.

If the original organization were described, one might hear the following description:

> In the beginning, the organization was designed simply to achieve basic and clearly defined goals. Its subsystems of authority, communications, incentives, and patterns of leadership were widely adopted as reasonable means to its goals. Its participants understood and accepted the roles, norms, and values as guides for acceptable individual behavior in merging individual efforts for the good of the organization. It was efficient and, under threat, sensitive to environmentally provoked needs for change.

Contrast this with a description of the new organization:

> Now the organizational arrangements are complex. Goals are diffuse and abstract. The organization must adopt and manage subsystems for such necessities as authority, communications, and incentives, which are uniquely designed to provide guidance for people working in groups with diverse activities and goals. Its participants accept their roles as they understand them. However, they may now be confused as to what manner of activity and level of productivity constitute acceptable behavioral patterns, particularly in merging individual contributions for the welfare of the entire organization. With nebulous goals, complex structure, complicated design of support subsystems, more highly specialized divisions of labor, and blurred definitions of acceptable roles, it is clear the organization will tend to be less efficient. And with situational security, it will also become less sensitive to needs for change.

The Aging Organization

During this final metamorphic stage of development, the organization of island castaways is not unlike many on-going, mature establishments. Over time, in a relatively placid environment, a social system will instigate rules, rituals, and other influences on participant behavior. As these social amenities are repeated, they become institutionalized. Such institutionalized patterns of behavior make up the cultural fabric, the social heritage of an organization. And people are hesitant to break with traditional ways of behaving. Even when behavior is grossly ineffectual and blatantly difficult, a person will commonly protect the status quo because at least there is comfort in knowing the task and security in understanding one's role relationship to others.

Rigidity

Thus, institutionalized arrangements tend to become fixed. As new goals and the means to achieving them become appropriate, they are imposed on the organization, but often without replacing long-standing behavioral patterns now grown obsolete. When abrupt, rather than evolutionary, changes are imposed on institutionalized behavior, internal inconsistencies tend to develop because certain systems of activity are not redesigned to support newly adopted goals.

Loss of Sensitivity

Further, as an organization becomes secure in its environment, it also becomes less sensitive to forces calling for change. It seems to become insulated from external forces and impervious to catalysts for change from within. Often, even after recognizing the need for a certain adjustment, it is lethargic in responding. This is understandable. In the absence of a threat to its security, there is little incentive to change.

The secure organization becomes more than only complacent. It inclines toward introspection, that is, it develops an overconcern with internal activities. Though natural, this can lead to further neglect of new developments in the external environment and divert energies from the pursuit of organizational goals. Organizational introspection is at work when large amounts of time and effort are used on activities having nothing to do with output, for example, political involvement; empire building; establishing "comfort zones" and taboos; harboring jealousy; and expressing pride, power, prestige, or position. Though it appears that it is natural for men and women to be so occupied, such activities can weaken organizational efficiency and effectiveness by (1) introducing internal inconsistencies (2) impeding alertness to the external environment and (3) diverting attention from the real competitor.

The organization now has lost the traits found in the original social system. Initially, a threatening situation gave rise to (1) explicit goals; (2) emergency of a cohesive, integrated social system; (3) internally consistent subsystems as means to goals; and (4) sensitiveness as well as

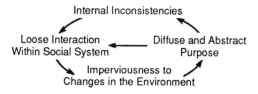

Figure III.A.6. Conceptual Model of Aging Organization

adaptiveness to environmental forces. Weigh now the traits of the current organization by examining the conceptual model in Figure III.A.6. The organization, though less cohesive than earlier, will continue to function, however, because it continues to fulfill the needs of its participants. It will, therefore, be supported until it demands more from its members than they believe they are getting from it.

Most organizations develop internal ambiguities and lose synchronization with their external situation, but they continue to function because they represent the best alternative available. Though cumbersome, they are our best or only means to goal achievement. We know how to manage an organization so that, through corrections, it can reach its goals in spite of its imbalances.

Demise of an Organization

Consider, finally, conditions that further weaken the bonds of integrated human effort, those that can lead to the ultimate demise of an organization so that the social system as it was formed ceases to function. You may recall that, unlike physical and physiological systems, when interaction stops the organization vanishes, leaving no remains other than the physical objects used during its existence. Physical and physiological systems, by contrast, leave structures that can be studied; these often provide explanations of the dynamics of the functioning organism and the reason for its failure. Unfortunately for students of organizations, no evidence remains of an organization's existence other than artifacts and historical records. These trappings usually are evidence of events, but often they do not reveal the causes of the disintegration of social arrangements. Thus, the study of organizational pathology is impeded.

The organization of our mythical marooned seafarers can be irreparably impaired in a number of ways. Among the more apparent reasons for collapse, the organization can lose sight of its goals; internal friction may become excessive and intolerable; the organization may fail to respond to new demands from either internal or external forces; or participants may feel that rewards are less than their contribution to the organized effort.

Pathology of an Organization

Let us now examine each of these causes of organizational illness in closer detail. Bear in mind that leaders of organizations must minimize these types of maladies if they are to preserve the continuing success of their enterprises. *Thus, recognition of these common hazards to organizational health lays the foundation for understanding the roles and goals of management.*

First, as agreement on common purpose wanes, the organization loses cohesiveness. With the goals of the enterprise more diffuse, abstract, and subject to personal interpretations, the social system loses structural sinew. Leaders are unable to develop and manage support subsystems when goals are not clearly defined. Participants are unable to see what behavior is acceptable. Leaders become indecisive in the absence of clearly stated aims against which alternatives must be weighed. Directives to subordinates lose effectiveness when they lack the "authority of the situation." Participants are unable to identify with organized efforts when the purpose of their efforts is clouded. In turn, involvement and dedication ebb. Then control is lost because goals are not there to set norms of performance against which actual contribution can be measured. All of these qualities lost are essential to organizational health.

Consider now how the individual voyagers will feel if the castaways' organization cannot be changed to meet new demands. Apprehensive members will seek a voice in the major decisions affecting their organization. Should its leaders continue to impose autocratic rule, subordinates will chafe because the situation no longer warrants such uncompromising behavior. Suppose the organization also grows impervious to demands from the external environment. Then, as a result, resources are wasted through overindulgence and contamination, shelters are inadequate to withstand tropical storms, and living areas become unhealthful through neglect. Confusion prevails as to appropriate roles, norms, and values. Coordination and integration are lost. The organization fades away and the group reappears—a loose assemblage of people engaged in casual interaction. As the trade-offs between inducements and demands widen in the eyes of participants, even casual arrangements weaken. Subgroups break away to seek self-maintenance through other arrangements. Finally, though the functional necessities of living are met in the fragmented groups, the original organization dies.

Summary

Though an unusual example, the islanders illustrate the unfolding life cycle of an organization. At its formation, or genesis, both the members and their organization are insecure; hence, they are sensitive to the need for change and responsive to these demands. The system is inefficient until coordination and refinement of its subgroups and processes are attained. During an organization's maturation, it tends to refine internal operations while continuing to be responsive to environmental forces. As it ages, organizational ills are caused by malfunction in one of three major areas: First, and most important, an organization cannot be managed without clear goals; second, an organization cannot be efficient when fraught with internal inconsistencies; and third, an organization cannot survive over time if it grows immune or unresponsive to changing environmental demands. The organization of the castaways was viewed as a dependent structure, part of an environmental system, where external forces had an impact upon the design and functioning of organizational arrangements. The approach has certain strengths. It encourages an examination of cause-effect reactions and the influence of sudden environmental changes on an organization. However, the major weakness in viewing an organization from this angle is its overemphasis on the passive, or reactive, aspects of organizational life. That is, some would point out that it unduly emphasizes adaptation while neglecting leaders' strategies to defy certain unfavorable external conditions. Others might claim that leaders can use their organizations' strengths as instruments to make external conditions compatible with their organizations. The approach used in the example of the shipwrecked party, some may say, neglects consideration of the leader's capacity to change environmental factors.

Most professional leaders, however, have little latitude to change basic environmental influences. They are nearly as confined in this respect as the head of the organization of shipwrecked survivors. The commander could do little to eliminate a shortage of food or threats from hostile inhabitants. Likewise, leaders in other enterprises can do little to change values, attitudes, philosophies, life styles, family sizes, or concentrations of populations. And these are the basic causal factors that influence organizational behavior. So most leaders—political, business, clerical, charitable, military, or whatever—react, rather than anticipate horizontal necessities for changes. They are concerned with appropriate, timely reactions to maintain their organizations' internal efficiency and external consonance.

Chapter IV

Systems Design

Design is the core of all professional training; it is 503 the principal mark that distinguishes the professions from the sciences. Schools of engineering, as well as schools of architecture, business, education, law, and medicine, are all centrally concerned with the process of design.[1]

Objectives

We have explored the potential of general systems theory and examined how to think productively about a specific type of system—the socio-technical organization. In this chapter, we narrow our focus to acquire the guidelines for designing an organization. Thus, we move from the abstract to the concrete, from theoretical concepts to practical application, from the academic "why" to the operational "how." But we will now be developing the tools for designing organizational systems with the aid of an invaluable insight: we know how we want the finished structure to look.

The goal is a production system, with its particular types of inputs, conversion, and outputs. In preparation for that challenge, let's work with the laws and principles that govern the design of systems. The preliminary step is somewhat like that of an architectural engineer mastering the conditions necessary for structural soundness, e.g. compression, tension, torque, stress, and strain, before attempting to design the plans for a house. He or she is obligated to ensure that the house will be structurally stable in the same way that designers of production systems are responsible for ensuring that their plan is capable of functioning properly. And these assurances—that the house won't fall down or the production system won't foul up—must be made *in advance* of their construction. So it seems worthwhile to acquire the intellectual "tools of the trade." The objectives of **Chapter IV** are:

- To understand what is involved in designing
- To comprehend the field of production systems
- To acquire "tools" for designing a system.

Introduction to Systems Design

Professional managers design organizations by using all the appropriate scientific discoveries. Thus, systems design is the art of applying scientific processes, techniques, ideas, and tools. It is a creative activity. If well done, the system that functions successfully can be immensely gratifying to its designers. And it should be, because the well designed system minimizes waste. It proclaims through action, not merely words, that management cares about the use of resources—materials, equipment, work area, and especially people.

In many organizations, systems evolve half by design, half by accident. But unlike living systems managed by long evolutionary processes, organizational systems have the potential for voids, redundancies, obsolescence, and incoherence. The people trying to function in a misdesigned organizational unit feel confused and frustrated, often to the point of anger or despair. Some resort to dysfunctional behavior to relieve their pain; others leave, or simply "drop-out" in a sort of on-the-job retirement. This occurs when internal arrangements (the system) prevent them from doing their jobs and reaching personal and organizational goals.

In a very real sense, the art of managing people can be reduced to answering this bedeviling question: *How do I keep from demotivating employees?* Everyone, after all, came to the organization motivated, often highly motivated, to serve. If not, why would they have been hired? Now the trick is keeping the people from "dropping-out." One essential way to meet that challenge is by designing efficient, internally consistent systems that demonstrate management's concern for employees and for other factors in the production process. Inefficiency—in systems design, or in any of its forms—*is* dehumanizing. Whether systems are intentionally designed to confound logic, or unintentionally permitted to drift into an incongruent state, the waste is the same. Systemic inefficiencies cause *systemic* behavioral problems.

Most successful managers manage systems more than they manage people. Given the mental, physical, and psychological qualities of today's employees, most of them will respond well to work demands if they are provided with support—systemic and interpersonal maintenance. In many organizational settings, therefore, the manager is well-advised to concentrate his or her intellect on the design of workable systems, and then to keep out of the way so that the people can do their jobs. In sum, if the system is basically sound, the manager can work to correct random deviations and to improve the system. If the system is unsound, the manager will be managed by the continuous fire-fighting activities required by the sweeping brush-fires of *legitimate* discontent. Most seasoned managers have in one setting or another felt the frustrations caused by bad organizational systems.

In this text, you are encouraged to develop the skills needed to design a new production system. The approach has merit, because it allows us to design an entire system (with interacting subsystems), an ideal plan. In another sense, the approach oversimplifies real-world conditions. Usually, people are assigned to manage ongoing systems. They "inherit" them. Some things about their newly-acquired operations are sound; other things are out of phase. The worst thing would be to enter a job believing that one must manage everything, re-do systems, personnel, and so on. The chances are high that many segments of the operation are good, while only specific phases are not. The newcomer, having developed a sensitivity to sound designs, will analyze the system and thus realign those elements or subsystems that have strayed. With a few managerial victories of this sort, other more sensitive changes will garner higher degrees of support from subordinates.

The Systems Design Process

The design process starts with a fully-drawn statement of the problem. This statement is of necessity bound-up with the goal, or goals, that the analyst wants the system to attain. The problem statement can easily be understated, or only partially drawn. For instance, a designer might view a production problem this way: "I want a system capable of producing 500,000 backpacks ready for marketing in six-months." With the problem so incompletely framed, a whole plethora of solutions—some relevant and many irrelevant—come to mind. Design a labor intensive system. Mechanized. Combined worker and machine. Batch. Process. Semi-automated. Fully automated. Subcontract the work. And so on. Which solution is correct? Until the statement of the production problem includes all essential conditions, we cannot know.

In reality, the issue is far larger than the mere production of 500,000 backpacks in six months. There are *essential* conditions that must be met, e.g. cost effectiveness, quality of the product, availability of inputs (plant, raw materials, machines, and people), financing, laws, and so on. The terse, incomplete definition of the problem misdirects the thinking

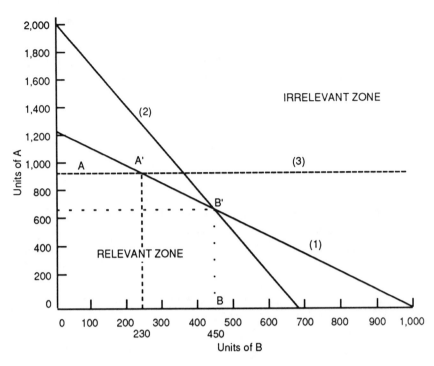

Figure IV.1. Linear Programming Graphic Solution

of an analyst and leads him or her to design impractical, perhaps unworkable, production systems.

Defining the problem verbally is analogous to defining a problem mathematically with the linear programming technique. In its most elementary use, a linear program presents conditions, called constraints, that impinge on a production problem and provides a graphic solution. Assume, for example, that we wish to optimize production of units of product A and units of product B. The goal is to maximize profits. Let us assume that each of the two products, A and B, contributes the same marginal amounts toward that goal. The obvious answer in Figure IV.1, if we ignore constraints for the moment, is to produce at the points on both axes farthest from the origin (0,0), i.e. at 2,000 units of A and 1,000 units of B. Yet this option becomes irrelevant if we consider the conditions that constrain production. There are shortages of time (constraint 1), skilled labor (constraint 2), and machine time (constraint 3). Since these conditions limit production of A as more units of B are produced at a constant rate, the only practical points at which to produce are along the constraints at the farthest distances from the origins, at point A, A', B', or B. To maximize output of units, we would automatically decide to produce at point A', where production of 1,000 units of A and 230 units of B is possible. For our purposes, the point of this example is as follows: until the constraints had been drawn, we had no rational basis for choosing a solution that would draw our thinking into the "Irrelevant Zone." It was not until essential constraints were imposed that thinking was forced to fit the fully-drawn problem within the "Relevant Zone." The design process starts with a fully-drawn statement of the problem.

The design process moves to consider all relevant solutions. Here begins the fun of exploration, the excitement of creativity. If the problem has been fully stated—excluding only the unfeasible solutions—*all* ideas can be raised for consideration within the "Relevant Zone." If not, some highly innovative approach to the design of the production system may fail to gain consideration. The possibilities are now bound only by *real* constraints (or timid imagination)—from exclusive use of labor to a fully automated plant, and all of the rich combinations in between that are available to design the most appropriate system.

When the total production system is being appraised, the analyst has a further opportunity. He or she can avoid the common tendency to limit the design to a few operations, and thus avoid becoming organizationally myopic.

> In a man/machine design, we tend to accept the fact of the machine and its output and question the motions used. At one system level higher in work systems, we tend to accept the system and the output but question the machines and their arrangements. Still another level higher in process analysis, we accept output but question the design of the constituent work systems.
>
> Why we need a machine, in other words, is *not* a legitimate question at the man/machine level, but *is* a legitimate question at the work system or process level.[2]

By being positioned to analyze and design the entire production system, the analyst can lead the inquiry into the way to organize to the limit of production/operations. The systems approach encourages the analyst to use his or her overall authority to pursue the total flow of the production process to the functional boundary, but not beyond it into other functional areas. The analyst is thus positioned to explore all relevant solutions from the top of the production function to the lowest level, unencumbered by limits to perspective or authority.

The design process now moves to an analysis of the strengths and weaknesses of relevant systematic solutions. The analyst now has a set of viable ways to design the production system; some labor intensive, some equipment intensive, others a combination of the uses of man and machine. Here, the analyst studies the various production options to find the most workable plan, given the fully-drawn statement of the problem. He or she will necessarily study and evaluate the overall workability of the systems proposed; the parts, elements, and subsystems; the way they interact; the size of equipment and inventories; and the timing of flows. As one systems authority puts it: "We consider the interconnections, the compatibility, the effect of one upon the other, the objectives of the whole, the relationship of the system to the users and the economic feasibility."[3]

This way of thinking—a systems way—is far more likely to find a solution than a study of the parts or the functional components standing in isolation.

This overview systems consideration means that it may become necessary to get preliminary cost estimates on the varied production options to find which ones are most feasible economically. If the decision rule for acceptance or rejection is cost effectiveness, these data are essential. If cost estimates are comparable, so that several options are economically feasible, another decision rule might be required, e.g. most innovative design, least risk of interruption to production, greater use of minorities or handicapped people, or development of loyalty among workers.

Both strengths *and* weaknesses of varied systems must be tested against some decision rule, or rules. The reader will discover that those who contribute ideas for specific approaches tend to see the virtues of their thinking, but are less sensitive (if not impervious) to the weaknesses. Yet all types of systems have both strengths and weaknesses. In production, sub-contracting may simplify internal arrangements, but increase costs and the risks of interrupted supply; a machine intensive plan may decrease the risk of strikes but increase lead-time and capital requirements; producing one's own raw materials decreases dependence on suppliers but increases investment, complexity, and risk. The astute systems analyst and designer expects feasibility studies of the varied ways of production to include strengths and weaknesses, benefits and costs, advantages and disadvantages, pros and cons—in the same way that any intelligent person has a need to learn of the major sides to issues. It is one mark of a truly productive thinker.

The selection of an integrated solution is made. After the strengths and weaknesses of options have been analyzed based on accepted decision rules, one system will stand out as most appropriate. This does not mean that other options are poor, but merely that the one selected best answers the production problem as framed and the criteria as chosen to form the decision rule. For instance, if goals are attainable in a set time by a number of systems proposed, and if the sole criterion for the selection is based on overall cost, then the system chosen will be the one that minimizes cost. No person needs to "win" over another, since the selection is based on objective criteria, not simple opinion.

Before making a final commitment to a specific system, the analyst must compare it to the definition of the production problem. On comparison, the final proposed production system must solve the production problem as it was originally defined with *all* of its essential conditions.

We have applied a modification of the *scientific approach, or method,* to the problem of selecting a production system. Let us now consider the field within which production systems function, and then move on to consider what is required for their management.

Interfaces of Production Systems

All systems to which man has been able to assign boundaries have fields of influences—e.g. man, organizations, societies, and earth. Production systems are bound by fields of influence or forces. In the immediate sense, these fields are other functional systems within the broader organization; in another sense these fields are represented by societal systems beyond the boundaries of the overall organization. Whether directly or indirectly, these two fields influence and are influenced by the production system. The points at which production relates to these fields are called *interfaces.*

Internal Interfaces

Within the organization, production interfaces with other closely related functional areas and authority levels. In a typical manufacturing company, production interfaces with other functional activities in a way that resembles the formal arrangements of the metals organization shown in Figure IV.2. A functional interface is shown on the same authority level between production and the vice president of marketing, vice president of engineering, treasurer, and controller. An authority interface

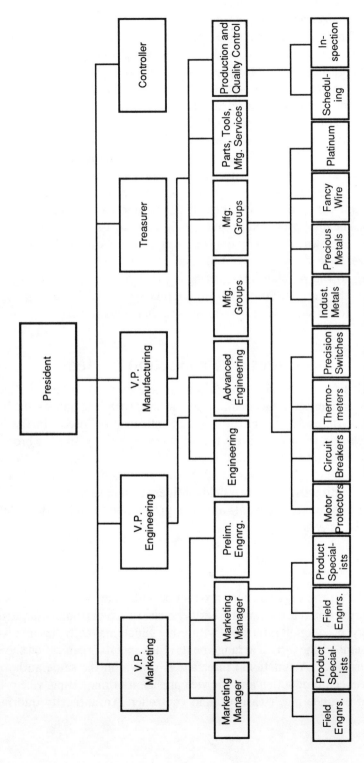

Figure IV.2. A Metals Organization

exists between all functional departments on the same authority level, with the president, who is responsible for overall company performance, on a superior level.

In other enterprises, other activities might be grouped into specialized units, e.g. legal, computering, public relations, or personnel. In such cases, the complexity of internal interface increases.

The interface phenomenon also occurs, of course, in enterprises that produce services rather than products. Whichever is produced, production systems are heavily influenced by their immediate environment—products are designed, legal restrictions imposed, personnel policies set, financing ascertained, safety requirements fixed, and certain controls levied. Thus, a production system is less open, more closed, than the overall organization. It is closed by constraints on its behavior.

External Interfaces

In a less immediate way, the production system interfaces with some of the same sources of influence faced by the overall organization. These forces are markets (particularly, product strategy), industry traditions, technology, social mores, public opinion (especially ecology and consumerism), legal climate (especially OSHA), and markets for labor, raw materials, and equipment.

These external interfaces, as well as those within the organization, pose constraints and offer opportunities to production, if management is able to listen and willing to respond appropriately.

Nature of Production Systems

By production system, we mean here the specialized process through which inputs are converted to outputs in the form of finished products or services that are different in kind from the inputs used. The production system could be a body shop, a pharmaceutical manufacturer, a plastics processor, a telephone company, a federal reserve bank, or another system producing something of value. Whatever is produced requires a common conversion process to transform input resources, the factors of production, into output.

The system has direct interfaces with related departmental functions within the overall organization. It also has less direct, or indirect, interfaces with a number of influencers outside the broader enterprise. With these facts in mind, we can define a viable production system as:

> A semi-closed socio-technical system of coordinated activities of people and/or machines designed to pursue goals by efficiently converting inputs to outputs, through internally consistent systems with each other and its goals, while adjusting to maintain a consonant interface with internal and external environments.

To design production systems, an analyst needs a schematic model as an overview to illustrate the relationships of inputs and their organization for output. In addition, the analyst requires a closer look at the specific elements that need to be considered to design a balanced system.

Conceptual Schematic Model (CSM)[4]

The Conceptual Schematic Model (CSM) in Figure IV.3 shows the overall sequential conversion process required to funnel the many inputs in a production system toward output. You will note that it incorporates major factors within the system and interfaces with extra-system influences. The model is primarily oriented to the operative production worker, but could be modified for service producers where no physical product is involved.

The conversion process is shown step-by-step, reading from left to right. It moves from output (1) backward through the processes necessary to marshall inputs (2–5), to the beginning point of gathering basic data from interface sources (6 and 7) in order to formulate ideas that act as a basis for designing production systems. The rectangles in the model represent major factors affecting output, circles connote influences between the major factors (1 and 2, 2 and 3), and hexagons show sources of data from internal and external interfaces (7). Solid lines point up heavy influences and dotted lines show weaker but nonetheless important influences.

CSM closely examines the way systemic and random factors impact on the output of a production worker.

Use of the CSM

CSM shows that efficient conversion of inputs and outputs is a function of three primary factors: the designed capacity of the task, the effort of individual workers, and interference beyond the control of the

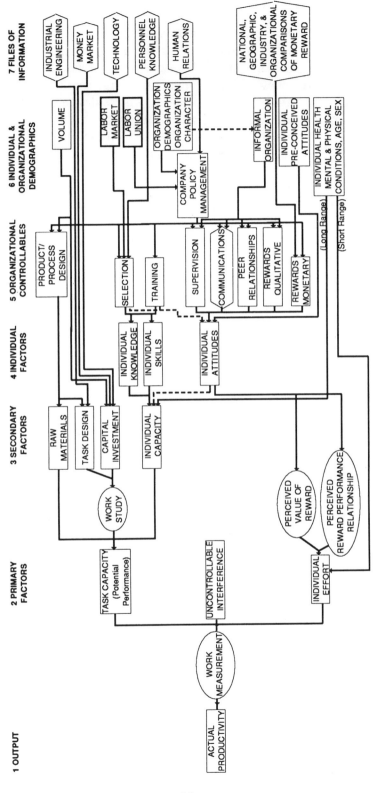

Figure IV.3. Conceptual Schematic Model

95

worker (2). Each of these primary factors is influenced, in turn, through secondary factors (3) that are designed based on data available on individual factors (4), including knowledge, skills, and attitudes. The chain of relationships continues through the design of organizationally controllable factors (5) that include product or process design, personnel selection, training, supervision, communications, peer relationships, monetary and non-monetary rewards, and company policy. At the outset, the production system is based on data about individual worker and organizational demographics (6), such as interfaces with the labor market, unions, and the nature of the worker, plus files of information (7) that furnish data on interfaces with such influences as engineering, technology, money markets, and industry trends.

The feature to study here—and the major contribution of the model—is that CSM presents the system of interacting variables on the conversion process in a complete, useful, and comprehensible way. CSM also points up that output is primarily caused by designed potential performance (task capacity), worker commitment (individual effort), and random variations from potential performance (uncontrollable interference). The challenge facing the system designer, therefore, is to coordinate source data and design controllables and secondary factors in such a coherent way that individual effort is increased to meet task capacity, with a minimum of interference from uncontrollable variations. Enter the classic systems design project, be it an automated hosiery plant, a world-wide agricultural monitoring network, a space colony, or a production unit.

Elements of Production Systems

We now have an overall perspective of the interacting system of variables required to produce efficiently. Now let us consider the key elements that shape the particular design of production systems. They include structures, hierarchies, processes, flows and stocks, trade-offs, and feedback.

Consider that you are asked as a production analyst to design a system to produce a backpack to be used for hiking. Through an interface with marketing, you find that it estimates that 1,200,000 units of the product depicted in Figure IV.4 can be sold for a price of $65.00 per unit, i.e. the market and pricing strategies are set. Further, industrial engineering, in conjunction with marketing, concurs that the product de-

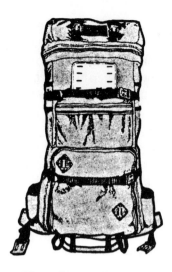

Figure IV.4. A BackPack

picted can be produced to meet market and price requirements. With these recommendations from related, interfacing functional units, the project gains top management support. You are asked by top management to provide a feasibility report in detail with the following instructions:

> Design a production system capable of producing 1,200,000 backpacks to be sold at $65.00 a unit with the specifications of the engineered prototype (a single original unit) accompanying this request by the date (two years in the future). Be certain that the system is clearly goal-oriented to meet the production deadline and internally consistent so that it is cost effective.

"Mission Impossible"? Not at all, if one begins by understanding the conditions surrounding the design project. At the outset, one knows that there are requirements that must be met by all production systems. In a curious way, these essentials simplify the design task.

Structure

There are certain impositions on the production of the product that convert an open system to one that is semi-closed.

Constraints. Constraints are conditions that are fixed and uncontrollable by the designer, at least in the short-run or foreseeable future.

They are sometimes called parameters. Since these are effectively immovable, the designer workers within them. They act as delimiting factors that map out the "Relevant Zone" for consideration as did the linear programming model shown earlier in this chapter.

The assignment to produce backpacks has four major constraints: Quality, quantity, deadline, and costs. As the designer, you know the limits of options available for your design.

Goals. The objective is clear: to produce 1,200,000 backpacks by a date two years hence through an internally consistent, cost-effective conversion system. The object, direction, and initial limits of your design have been provided.

Resources. All production systems need inputs, or resources. To produce the backpacks will require the typical resources of land, buildings, labor, machines, and raw materials. Yet, since it is implied that the planned production system is but a part of a larger on-going enterprise (a subsystem from the president's viewpoint), resources required will be financed by the broader organization.

This condition simplifies matters, of course, since the designer need not be concerned with the acquisition of capital. It does mean, however, that the production system designed will be responsible and responsive to a number of interfacing units—engineering, controller, legal, computer center, and perhaps, personnel—within the broader organization. The requirements exacted by these functional areas can act as added constraints. At the minimum, they require close interaction.

Hierarchies

We know from our study of general systems and organizational systems that some framework or structure is necessary in all systems. In many systems, as in production, hierarchies provide the skeletal framework within which organic subsystems function and can be modified.

Technological. Producing 1,200,000 backpacks requires a relatively simple, yet critically important, technology. The hierarchy is based on the amount of money spent or invested. You may elect to design a system where land, building, sewing machines, and tube molders are at the top of the ranking while hand tools, grommets, screws, and paperclips are at the bottom.

The systems designer knows that this hierarchy is essential, and plans to get data on production configuration, physical facilities, and purchasing to ensure that no required part of technology is omitted.

Financial. The production system will develop a financial structure, or hierarchy. At the top may be major capital investments for technical resources such as heavy machinery or buildings; leases for land or equipment may follow in size of outlay; these may be followed by wages and operating expenses for hand tools and parts, with incidental random expenses at the bottom of the hierarchy. The designer will know that accountability for this hierarchy of financial structure is as important as the inventory of the hierarchy of technology. Thus, he or she will be acutely aware of the need for determining expenditures throughout the design process. These costs must be well below the total revenues from the sales of the backpacks, if the venture is to be profitable.

Raw Materials. Producing backpacks, or any other product or service, requires a hierarchy of raw materials. The ranking begins with the materials most important to the finished product—for backpacks, extruded aluminum tubing, then canvas, webbing, buckles, down to lacing, and grommets. There can be no void in this hierarchy. For scarce, essential items, the availability of alternate suppliers is prudent. You, as analyst, can develop this important data from scheduling, inventory, and production control.

Human. As well as a technical and financial system, production is a human social system. The hierarchy of human relationships is based on authority ranking. All organizations require formal ranking to affix accountability, without overly burdening individuals. The ranking to produce backpacks may begin with a production/operations manager at the top, with intermediate managers, supervisors, and staff specialists in the mid-zone, down to seamstresses, metal fabricators, assemblers, and warehouse workers at the lowest operation level. The hierarchy is designed based on information on methods of production, personnel or labor, and the overall organizational structure of the production system.

Process

Process refers to the methods by which raw materials, equipment, and human skills are transformed into product or service outputs. As system designer, you make the process selection.

Conversion. In all production systems, materials and energies are converted into a product or service output. There are a number of types of conversion processes available to a system designer. With the production of backpacks, one may select a batch throughput strategy because of the specific numbers of units to be produced, the high ratio of

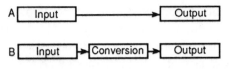

Figure IV.5. Input-Output Models

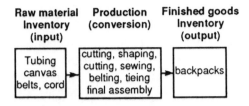

Figure IV.6. Input-Output Model of BackPack Production System

human resource usage to machine usage and, especially, the varied types of sub-processes required to complete backpacks. One unit may be cutting, shaping, and coating aluminum tubing for frames; another unit may be cutting and sewing canvas packs; a third may be assembling and packing the finished products, largely from semi-finished material supplied by other units.

Input-Output Model. In its most elementary form, the notion of systemic input-output would assume the form of A in Figure IV.5 with no change from input to output by the system—merely a conduit. But if we add the idea of conversion in the same graphic, B, it then conveys the more realistic representation that outputs are indeed converted from the nature of the inputs.

In the instance of producing backpacks, therefore, the input—conversion—output model acquires the form shown in Figure IV.6. Scheduling, purchasing, inventory, and production control become entities to ensure that there is a balanced flow throughout the input—conversion—output sequence.

Interactions.[5] When a certain process, or combination of processes, is considered, thought should also be given to the design of tasks. Here, there are interactions between the man/machine and assembly line, or "batch processes", that have a definite influence on the efficiency, i.e. effectiveness, of the system. For instance:

> If the task design is inherently/systemically/inefficient, clumsy, and displeasing to the individual, the person may exert less effort that he would in a more satisfying task. On the other hand, if a task is so

streamlined, specified, and standardized that it is dehumanized, the individual may rebel . . . withdraw, or turn to dysfunctional activities. The task design may also interact with the peer relationship in some cases. Designing tasks as a moving assembly line can change the effect on the individual or peer relationships. Tasks that are group oriented and designed to be interdependent in process tend also to cause the workers of the group to become interdependent socially; in this case the peer relationships would be extremely strong in determining the actual productivity.[6]

The batch process was chosen to produce backpacks for technical reasons. That process relies heavily on peer control. Thus, in choosing workers, personnel must take care to select people who are outgoing, principled, and self-starting. As system designer, you will want close coordination here among the task design, or methods, manpower, and organizational dimensions of the system. Otherwise, malfunctional behavioral relationships could easily result.

Feedback

Feedback is a form of information periodically received at varied stages of the conversion process to ascertain if actual output conforms to standards of desired output. "An information feedback [sub]system exists whenever the environment leads to a decision that results in action which affects the environment."[7] The production of goods and services (output) is done to fill a need or want in the marketing environment. The final configuration of goods and services impact at the interface on that consumer environment, making a feedback loop necessary to inform production if output meets user expectations. Decisions based on that feedback of information will, in turn, affect production and, ultimately, customers served in the environment.

Cybernetics Model. For centuries the word cybernetics has been used to mean feedback for control: To Plato, cybernetics was the science of steering ships; later, to Ampere, the science of controlling society; still later, to Weiner, the science of control and communications in animals and machine;[8] and now, to systems designers, the science of comparing output to standards for control. In all production systems, cybernetic loops are designed into the system in their most elementary form as shown in Figure IV.7.

Here, the basic structure over which output is measured by a feedback channel is displayed, so that actual performance can be compared to and contrasted with desired performance. Once done, decisions are

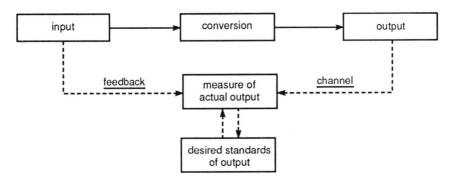

Figure IV.7. Cybernetic Control Subsystem

made to affect input and bring about desired output. And the cybernetic control subsystem—a servosystem—continues its monitoring to provide data for future adjustments.

The model presented above is a theoretically sound control mechanism, but it over simplifies the design of control systems in two major ways: first, control is needed throughout the conversion process, not simply at the point of output; and second, controls for varied specialized factors—quality, quantity, raw material usage, machine settings, and so on—are required, not merely one general control of inputs.

For example, if you are to control the production of backpacks using a batch process for cutting and shaping tubing, cutting and sewing canvas, and final assembly, you will wish to design checkpoints for each of these subprocesses, in addition to the final inspection of the output, the completed backpack. Further, you will want to be assured that various types of standards are maintained to ensure a certain quality, a calibrated quantity, machine maintenance, and a minimum of wasted materials or labor hours. The control model, similar to the one shown in Figure IV.7, will be used at various points in the conversion process for various types of control. It would be reasonable for the process of producing backpacks that fifteen to twenty such models might be designed and installed into the production system as parts of the control subsystem.

A number of subsystems are intimately involved. Standards are set by those responsible for the configuration—the production design—of the product. In addition, scheduling, purchasing, methods, inventory, quality control, and production control affect and are affected by the subsystem for control.

Stocks and Flows. All complex systems have inputs that circulate through them—whether the system is the human body, a car engine, the national economy, or a production unit. They are either concentrated in reservoirs or storage points, or they circulate through the system. If the inputs, say, are at storage points, they are stocks awaiting use; if the inputs are moving through the system, they are flows being used. In the automobile, for instance, gasoline is a stock awaiting use when the engine is off. But when the engine is running, part of the stock is a flow to permit internal combustion. We measure the stock by tank capacity, e.g. full, half-full, or empty—a measure of absolute volume. We account for the flow by miles per gallon—a measure of relative rate.

In production systems, recognition of the difference between stocks and flows of inputs is essential, because they must be planned. This is analogous to the motorist planning a trip across a desert with a long distance between service stations. The driver must plan the trip with concern for both the *stock* of gasoline in the tank and also the *rate* of flow of expected use. If the rate of use per mile in sum exceeds tank capacity, the driver will take on an extra supply in a gas container to ensure reaching his destination. In a similar way, systems designers are aware of the stocks and flows of inputs required to reach their goals.

The system designed to produce backpacks has a number of stocks and flows of various inputs. An adequate supply of the many inputs is planned so that they accumulate for future use in raw materials inventory, move at a rate of use through goods-in-process (conversion), and finally end (if there is no wastage) in another stock called finished goods inventory. Finally, the finished goods stock is drained by the rate of flow of backpacks to markets. Note: when we say that production systems designers must plan for an "adequate supply," the meaning of "adequate" is determined by an awareness of the rate of input use. Figure IV.8 traces the stocks and flows of inputs. If you designed the inventory subsystem to produce backpacks, valuable source data to determine necessary stocks and flows would be gathered from purchasing, methods, scheduling, production control, quality control and physical facilities.

Trade-Offs

The design of a production system inevitably involves trade-offs; that is, attaining one system feature means that another feature must be given up. Trade-offs are a natural part of the give and take—or "iterative process"—of system design. It is indeed this reconciliation through trade-offs that can bring about internal consistency, balance, and cost effectiveness. This can occur if the designers are willing to integrate, to sub-optimize, to compromise for the benefit of the *overall* system.

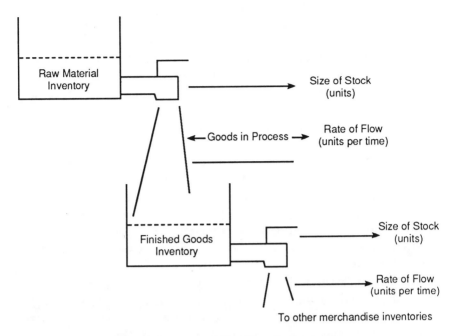

Figure IV.8. Stocks and Flows in a Production System

Consider some of the trade-offs required to balance the production system for backpacks. A higher investment in labor-saving machines will mean less labor, fewer methods of task design, and perhaps fewer raw materials. You may be confronted by a trade-off between make-or-buy decisions. A trade-off may be required between hiring skilled personnel at high wages and hiring unskilled people for training within. Some may want a highly complex, sophisticated system for quality control that could easily decrease cost effectiveness. The scope of the potential trade-offs in system design encompasses all subsystems. The intensity of feelings about making trade-offs (especially among sincere technical experts) is often great. Yet trade-offs are essential.

Summary

This chapter addresses itself directly to designers of production systems. It presents the design process and the interfaces between production systems and influencers on production—both within the organizational system and outside it, in the environment.

The nature and definition of production systems are provided. A Conceptual Schematic Model (CSM) is presented to show the complexity of a production system, the subparts, and the relationship of the parts to the broader system and its capacity to produce output.

Attention is then narrowed to the elements that shape the design of systems for production. The influences of structure, hierarchies, process, feedback, stocks and flows, and trade-offs are presented. Here, for the first time, the reader is encouraged to think about these conditions as the designer of a production system—goal-seeking, internally consistent, and cost effective—for a specific product.

Notes

1. Herbert A. Simon, *The Sciences of the Artificial* (Cambridge, Massachusetts: The MIT Press, 1970), pp. 55–56.
2. Leroy H. Mantell, "The Systems Approach and Good Management," *Business Horizons,* October, 1972, pp. 43–51.
3. Jay W. Forrester, *Industrial Dynamics* (Cambridge, Massachusetts: The MIT Press, 1961), pp. 5–6.
4. The following presentation of the Conceptual Schematic Model is based on William A. Ruch and James C. Herschauer's *Factors Affecting Worker Productivity* (Tempe, Arizona: Bureau of Business and Economic Research, Arizona State University, 1974), pp. 27–33.
5. *Ibid.* Based on a discussion from pp. 31–32.
6. *Ibid.*
7. Jay W. Forrester, "The Impact of Feedback Control Concepts on the Management Sciences" (Distinguished Lecturer, October 26, 1960, Foundation for Instrumentation, Education, and Research, New York).
8. John A. Beckett, *Management Dynamics: The New Synthesis* (New York: McGraw-Hill Book Company, 1971), p. 76.

Part II

Systems Management

Beginning with **Chapter V, Part Two** applies systems concepts as an engineering manager would apply them in a simulated production planning department. As a consequence, the intellectual and behavioral experiences of both the manager and the designers are recounted.

The study of socio-technical systems is expanded in **Part Two** to the overall enterprise of which the production/operations syystems is a part—a subsystem. A synthesis is a combination of parts, elements, or subsystems to form a whole. Thus, to synthesize management systems, **Chapter VI** considers the dynamic interrelationships within a production/operations subsystem. The dual challenges of the manager—as system stabilizer and change agent—are explored. The need for internal consistency is examined as a means to efficiency. But even efficient operations fail if their managers are unable or unwilling to generate bonds of cohesion to connect their units to the broader enterprise and its environment. These essential interfaces are the major focus. **Chapter VII** contemplates the consequences of system failures to the individual and society.

Chapter V

Managing Systems Design

Systems analysis employs a systems approach, but using a systems approach in system design is easier said than done.[1]

Objectives

The last four chapters presented the ideas of general systems, system components, organizational systems, and systems design. We admit that the notions so introduced do not take on full meaning until they are applied. To design a production system, however, a manager must be aware of the models available as aids to guide decisions. We are now prepared to consider the processes and behavioral aspects of managing the design of a production system.

The role of the manager here is complex and important. The basic work involves analysis of the overall design, synthesis of subsystems, and evaluation of predicted outcomes in performance and cost effectiveness. Beyond the basic tasks, the manager must accommodate inputs from varied specialists and integrate their ideas so that a balanced total plan is produced. Thus, both the process and people are crucial to a successful design.

This chapter has the following objectives:

- To provide the management concepts needed to manage a design staff
- To present the essential processes required to design a balanced production system.
- To discuss the human behavior displayed by system designers

Introduction

Many progressive organizations have a "planning organization" made up of professional planning staffs. These are often called corporate planning, project team, or perhaps, business planning. They are groups of specialists whose role is to initiate new ways of doing things, to facilitate, review, evaluate, and consult with management. They usually recommend systems designs for top management approval and for lower management implementation. These units therefore serve as a source of highly skilled experts in a capacity as functional/planning/advisory staffs.

In all complex organizational systems there is the need for system planning and design. This function must be fulfilled with or without formal institutional arrangements such as a planning unit. The functional need is often filled by less formal means, such as standing planning committees or loosely bound groups of key people. The reader should be aware that, in organizational systems in which functional necessities are required, voids are intolerable. Someone must fill the essential niche by assuming the responsibility for getting the job done. Such informality can cause problems. The persons assuming the responsibilities may not possess the necessary perspective, or viewpoint; they also may not have the appropriate authority, and may not be held accountable. To avoid these problems, enlightened leaders make certain that the management of systems design is formalized. In the planning of the design of a production system, specialists from such areas as product design, industrial engineering, and industrial management could represent the nuclear group—with a manager of systems design in charge.

Whatever the form, someone or some group must be accountable for nurturing "a strategic system planning culture"[2] in which the following fundamentals are converted from policies to operational definitions:

> *First,* a sense of purpose is required in the organization—a desire to objectively determine what "business" the organization is in, what business the organization should be in, and a strategy for delineating how the organization will get where it wants to go.

> *Second,* a commitment to a participative management style is necessary—the development of a *culture* in the organization which facilitates a high degree of participation in the development of strategies and develops people's capacities and will to eagerly seek and enjoy the challenges of the strategic systems planning process.

> *Finally,* a recognition that planning is important must permeate the organization—an accepted and demonstrated belief on the part of the organizational managers that strategic systems planning is important and valued within the organization and that people will be rewarded for their success in developing future strategies.[3]

These statements are extended beyond their pontifical tone when they are made operational by the design manager and his or her planning unit.

The Design Manager

The design manager in production is responsible ultimately for the final recommendation of the way a product or service will be produced. This responsibility is met by marshalling his or her knowledge of systems with active participation from staff members. The design goal is reached by the manager who can orchestrate processes and people.

Perspective

The manager of the design process must have a full view of the area of activity that requires systemic design, as well as an awareness of essential interfaces. This field of reference, which includes all factors and constraints affecting the system, provides an adequate, essential vantage point. As we have seen, for example, if the manager is responsible for the design of the organizational system, a view from the top and a sense of the broader external environment is required. If a manager is designing a production system, a perspective on all manufacturing units and subsystems is essential, as is an awareness of production's interfaces with other functional areas inside and relevant interfaces outside the enterprise. If a manager is to design a subset of the production system, say the purchasing subsystem, he/she must have an overview of all aspects of purchasing, together with an appraisal of internal interfaces, such as inventory control, and cost control. In addition, the manager must be attuned to external interfaces, such as supply and demand forecasts, consumerism, ecology, safety, and ethical conduct, which impose constraints and provide opportunities for the overall purchasing subsystem.

The perspective required can be thought of graphically by considering Figure V.1. At the lower levels of the production department the people are largely concerned with the technical and behavioral skills required to manage and operate the system after it has been designed. They are system managers. At the upper level of perspective, the people are concerned essentially with conceptual and behavioral skills needed to manage the design of a system that is operationally sound. You will

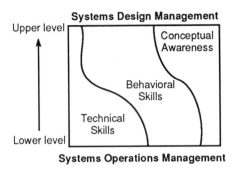

Figure V.1. Perspectives of System Design and Operations. (Source: An adaptation of an illustration by Keith Davis, *Human Behavior at Work,* 4th ed. (New York: McGraw-Hill Book Company, 1972), p. 107.)

note that managing the design of a production system requires a perspective sufficiently expanded to include important interfaces and grasp of the technical skills that is detailed enough to create a workable design.

Skills

We might consider the perspective of the manager of systems design in one further way to point up the skills required. Many experts in production management view it as a process, a process through which a manager plans, organizes, directs, and controls inputs and the conversion process. At the lower levels of production, the people are mostly concerned with directing and controlling manufacturing activities. At the upper levels, the people are primarily involved in planning and organizing the production system. Stated another way, lower level people are managing and operating the system by directing and controlling activities. At higher levels, the people are designing the system by planning and organizing. Figure V.2 illustrates this point.

By placing Figures V.1 and V.2 together, we can see that, to operate a production system, one needs technical and behavioral skills to direct and control manufacturing activities. It also becomes clear that the person managing the design of a production system requires a conceptual overview and behavioral skills if he/she is to be able to plan and organize the system. An important but less obvious point, is this: if a person advances from lower operative levels to higher design levels, an intellectual and psychological change, a metamorphosis, must take place if the person is to acquire the perspective needed to design broader, more complex systems.

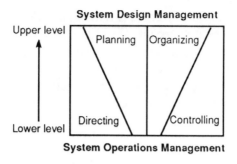

System Design Management

Upper level ⬆ Lower level

Planning   Organizing
Directing   Controlling

System Operations Management

Figure V.2. The Processes Perspective of System Design and Operations. (Source: An adaptation of a visual presentation by George R. Terry, *Principles of Management,* 6th ed. (Homewood, Ill.: Richard D. Irwin, Inc., 1972) p. 87.)

In sum, successful designers of production systems possess:

1. An understanding of the technology of their production processes
2. An understanding of the basic processes and concepts of sound management
3. An interpersonal behavioral style that facilitates getting things done through others
4. An ability to conceptualize and to use a systems approach.[4]

Role[5]

Role means the part people play in the organization. The design manager's role is thereby the organizational part played by the person who formally influences the behavior and activities of other people in the design process and, as a consequence, affects the behavior of the planning unit. The role is given legitimacy and authority because the person acquiring the managerial position is fulfilling functions needed by members of the planning staff. Let's examine those essential management functions.

First, managers set, define, and communicate the purpose, goals, or ends of organizational effort. This is basic to integrated, coordinated, and directed activity, whether the organization is a shoe-shine stand, General Motors, a commune, a kibbutz, or an army. Purpose is communicated by action and symbolism as well as words. To be effective, purpose needs to be accepted by those contributing to its fulfillment. As we have asserted earlier, this means that "it must be redefined in terms of specific objectives for specialized units."[6]

Second, managers design (most commonly redesign) the overall social system and its subsystems of operating relationships to encourage participants to strive for their part in the organization's goals. All joint human endeavors require subsystems for orderly operations. John A. Beckett observes:

> Rock groups, dance bands, symphony orchestras, athletic teams, committees, governments, and innumerable others offer ample additional evidence that even in organizations that consist exclusively of people, management is achieved largely through the instrumentality of a *system* of operating relationships . . . In the case of music and athletic groups, for example, it is the system that enables the activity to be operated through the development of individual skills and through exhaustive rehearsal and practice of the group.[7]

Managers anticipate a variety of conditions and design the overall system and its related parts so that needed operating relationships can flourish.

Third, managers act as catalysts to induce reactions that will propel the system toward its goals. Since a manager's influence is brought to bear on the total structure, he or she serves both as system catalyst and regulator. The sound manager cannot exert random force on the organization, or induce behavior in one part to the jeopardy of others, or expect results from individuals that the system will not tolerate. This would be similar to reversing gears in a forward moving car only to find that the car has been damaged because the mechanized system cannot adjust. To make corrections or changes, the entire fabric of operating relationships must be considered.

Fourth, managers design and redesign systems to bring about internal consistency. Systems largely do the managing. It is unrealistic to believe that managers manage an organization. In truth, "the organization as a whole manages itself."[8] At the least, the subsystems manage stability, continuity, and control.

Fifth, and last, managers interpret environmental forces; translate their impact upon the organization; design changes that appear appropriate to cope with the changing environment; and implement the changes through adjustments in goals, means, and subsystems of activity. An organization must adjust constantly to both internal and external forces. Managers (or more completely, the hierarchy of managers) are the nerve center of the enterprise. Part of a manager's role is to sense the need to adjust and to initiate appropriate action.

In sum, a manager's role includes the traits of innovator to establish and communicate purpose, systems designer, leader or catalyst, systems regulator and boundary mediator, and agent for change.[9] We can now summarize the manager's role as a functional requirement of the organization.

Basic Organization Needs	Basic aspects of the Manager's Role
1. Common purpose	1. Establish and communicate purpose
2. Social system and subsystems	2. Design systems and subsystems
3. Catalyst to place system into motion and maintain cooperation	3. Give direction
4. Internal consistency	4. Systems regulator, boundary mediator, and stabilizer for efficiency
5. Environmental consonance	5. Sensing and change agent for viability and long-run effectiveness

The Processes of a Design Department
A Simulation

The process of designing a production system is the sequential flow of activities required from the beginning to end. A simulation is a representation of reality. In this instance, we will verbally and graphically simulate the major steps to be taken in the design process of a real-world production system.

To do so, the reader must imagine that his or her department will be transformed into a functional production systems planning department. Let's call it "Super Integrated Systems Design Department." Remember, this department is made up of *your* people. No one outside is eligible.

Your unit—Super Integrated Systems Design Department—is a part of a corporation that produces a number of products and services. It is a progressive company that responds quickly to provide its outputs

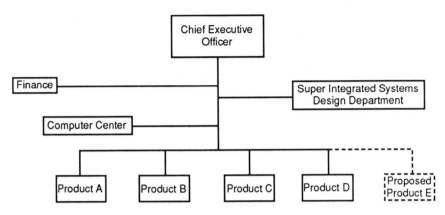

Figure V.3. Formal Organization

profitably to changing markets. The firm has diversified the products and services it produces to decrease its reliance on the sales of a single output—in a word, to cut risk. It markets outputs through exclusive agents, leaving the company in the primary position of designing, financing, and managing superior production systems. That is its major competitive strength. Your Design Department is positioned organizationally as shown in Figure V.3. You can see that it is accountable to top management, with support interfaces with finance and the computer center. Proposals for potentially lucrative new products are received by the Chief Executive Officer (CEO) from marketing agents. The CEO refers them to you as Manager of the Design Department as Request for Quotes. In return, the CEO expects to receive a comprehensive, thorough analysis of the issue and a recommendation for the design of a cost-effective, workable (i.e. goal attainable) production system. In this case, the system that you and your subordinates design based on the Request for Quote may become the Product E Production System shown in Figure V.3.

Action in the Design Department is triggered by receipt of the Request for Quote from the CEO. Let us assume that it involved the product—backpacks—introduced in Chapter IV and a similar form reintroduced here in Figure V.4.

You and your associates have been challenged. Now let's consider the processes that you might experience in the "design department."

TO:	Manager of Super Integrated Systems Design Department
FROM:	Chief Executive Officer
SUBJECT:	Request for Bid—Backpacks
REFERENCE:	Original, follow-up in eight to ten weeks

The Lucrative Marketing group believes that backpacks can be profitably sold if (1) their introduction to the market is well timed, and (2) they can be produced in a cost-competitive way.

Provide a quote to my office by (eight to ten weeks hence) that includes a detailed analysis of a workable production system capable of producing 1,200,000 backpacks to be sold at $65.00 per unit meeting the specifications of the prototype accompanying this request. The total production run must be ready for marketing within two years. The key to your analysis is that the production system designed be clearly capable of meeting that production goal, and that all parts be internally consistent so that it is cost effective.

If you have questions see my coordinator, Mr. Goodwrench.

Figure V.4. Request for Bid Memo

Goal. The conditions for the goal of the department can be loosely inferred from the Request for Bid memo. But you note that the Bid may require a 150 to 200 page analysis to include the overall system, subsections for each integrated subsystem, and a comprehensive cost evaluation. Most challengingly, all subsystems must be balanced to support each other and the goal of producing 1,200,000 units within two years. (whew!)

You can envision that sub-reports will be required for the following subsystems integral to the overall system for production:

Product configuration   Inventory control
Scheduling   Quality control
Physical facilities   Production control
Purchasing   Organization
Labor   Costing
Job design

The goal is to produce a thorough design, and a realistic cost estimate that includes a comprehensive bid.

Constraints. Three noteworthy constraints come quickly to mind: Time, people (resources), and technical knowledge (perhaps, even managerial skills). This major report is due in eight to ten weeks. There are only your technical experts, 20 to 30 people, to design it. And, they have only limited technical knoweldge of the specific system required to produce backpacks.

Point of Departure. To design a system one needs a point of departure—a break-in point. When designing to produce a product or service, that critical point is a detailed analysis of the configuration of the product or service. Here, all will look to the engineers in the Production Configuration subgroup for the nomenclature of the product to guide their activities.

Subgroup Activities. With the charge made to produce a design and the product intellectually (sometimes, physically, dissected), the subgroups at first hesitantly, then forthrightly, respond to the task at hand. Though they sense the interdependence of it all, they try to function reatively independently, at the outset.

A flurry of ideas are generated within each subgroup. In the purchasing subgroup (used here merely as one example of eleven available), one member thinks that production should produce a certain part of the final product, another believes it should be purchased, while yet another member wants to subcontract its acquisition. Who is correct? They don't know at this point because the overall strategy and decision criteria have not been provided.

Research. Subgroup members conduct research to find the best techniques. In quality control, as one example, technologists acquire sound sampling techniques from books and articles by authorities. They might simulate points in the conversion process where checkpoints seem prudent. They may check with local producers of products similar to the backpack to learn of their quality control subsystem. Whatever the sources of the files of technical knowledge, they search it out.

The reader may recall that earlier limited sources of "technical knowledge" caused us to consider it a constraint, or limitation, on the design of the system. We now find that the technical skills can be acquired and can therefore be considered a variable—and a manageable variable. By this we mean that if technical knowledge is not readily available to staff members, they can be directed to learn it so that its loss does not impair the quality of the design.

Iterations. Iterations are the means by which the ideas from subgroups are tested for appropriateness by other interfacing subgroups those ideas affect. For instance, an idea from the production control subgroup that seems to be needed to ensure a smooth cadence of conversion will be tested against ideas by such interfacing subgroups as purchasing, quality control, and inventory control to find if the notion is workable. Often, this testing leads to modifications of ideas so that they will "fit" smoothly with those of the designers of other subsystems.

It should be noted that iterative processes, and resultant decisions, cannot be made productively without someone administering the overall design against agreed-upon criteria, such as lowest cost or highest quality.

Control. Control is essential in the Design department if subgroup outputs are to be timely, of sufficiently high quality, and calibrated with the outputs of other subgroups toward the goal of a design that will get the production job done. The control point, to be effective, must come from an authority source above the level of subgroup leader, because each subgroup leader is vying to maximize his/her particular function, not optimize system performance.

Priorities. The manager can now determine what assignments must logically precede and influence other assignments. He or she can schedule the unfolding logical flow of output from each subgroup, beginning with product configuration, and orderly working through other subgroups, to end with costing.

Trade-offs. The manager soon learns that to accept one way of proceeding means giving up another. Trade-offs are a necessary part of the process to smooth, calibrate, balance. Absolutes vanish in the design of a complex system. The manager gets the uneasy feeling that comes when attempting to reach delicate balances—balancing human involvement and human ideas, such as:

Man and machine
Conflict, cooperation and compromise
Competition and cooperation
Traditional and innovative
Overall goal and subgroup goals
Output and organizational maintenance
Equity and debt
Quantity, quality, time use, and costs
Formal and informal interaction
Autocracy and participation
Empathy and objectivity
And on and on[10]

The leader is involved in weighing trade-offs, where a sound overall design hinges on balancing these issues plus many others.

Optimum Balance. The system designer strives to attain an optimum balance in the production system. By optimum balance, we mean a coordinated design that is as efficient as the constraints imposed on its design will tolerate. Optimizing differs from maximizing efficiency and output. No system probably can maximize performance. The car engine is subject to friction. The human system can only store so much energy. The economic system is fraught with structured institutional sluggishness. And, the maximization of production system is limited by such conditions as limited suppliers, shut-downs for maintenance, and social norms about work. As a chain is only as strong as its weakest link, *a system is only as efficient as its least efficient subsystem.* Otherwise, balance would be lost. The key issue for the designer is to recognize real constraints, and then to design the production system to the furthest point of sub-maximization, which is optimization.

We have simuated what would likely take place if a planning unit were charged with designing a production system. Let us now trace a sequence of the process in Figure V.5 that might prove to be a sound way of proceeding.

Human Behavior in a Simulated Design Department[11]

The experience in the simulated design department provides a rich wealth of learning for a member. The participant will develop deeper insights into the technical knowledge and conceptual awareness required to design a production system, of course. But beyond this, he or she will

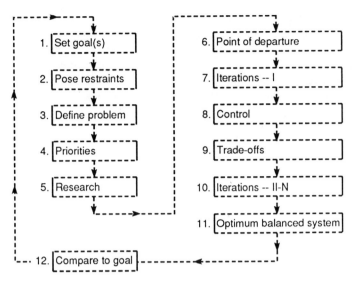

Figure V.5. Process of a Simulated Design Department

become aware of the human behavior experienced in the process of systems design—the necessity for formal organizational arrangements, the strengths and weaknesses of informal arrangements, and the feelings accompanying interpersonal relationships.

Systems Thinking

Learning to think in systems terms, for all its virtues, has formidable obstacles. You will see clearly that there is meaning to recognizing constraints, feedback, homeostasis, cybernetics, and perhaps even that cumbersome word, equifinality. You may also be comforted to be told what you had always suspected, that everything is somehow related to everything else. Yet, once the ideas are learned, what does one do with them? How does one gain practical merit from those intellectual artifacts? Stated more abruptly, "so what?" That is an understandable and fair question that can be answered only by applying the newly-found skills. Here are revelations by technical specialists who used the systems approach:

> "I gained a deeper understanding of what makes a system function
> and the problems that must be dealt with through human effort,
> participation, and interaction."

121

"I got a greater and first-hand look at what really happens in the processes it must go through to become efficient. It (the experience) turned out to have very practical applications of both the knowledge gained earlier, e.g. management, personnel, and human relations." "I realized the great practical applications of systems theory learned earlier." "It (the simulation) gave me an opportunity to use what the system design was all about."

And, that last statement is what a simulated experience *is* "all about."

Formal Organization

There are those people who continue to resist being organized, or having their behavior structured. Yet, alas, those who experience the operation of a simulated systems design department permit their zeal for self-determination to fade into the background, while their newly-acquired awareness of organizational necessities comes to the fore. Here are some comments from engineers that express their discoveries, better than we can convey them:

"Cooperation alone won't cut it!" . "Informal leaders may be O.K. They will emerge, but when the going gets tough they can also submerge." . "Unless someone is assigned accountability formally, another will end up doing all the work." . "It takes a lot of energies to organize and control a group of people, *even* though they (ostensibly) have the same goal." . "The main thing I learned was that no matter how much you learn about delegation that if you're a leader and something goes wrong, you get the worst part of it." . "I witnessed a lot on how the formal organization comes alive." . "I got a general view of all that is required to get an organization off the ground, but we wasted a h___ of a lot of time trying to figure out who was doing what and when."

Formally organizing the human resources of the design department may not be as cordial as depending on informal cooperation, but it's the only way to achieve the goal(s) unless we have an inexhaustible supply of resources, i.e. no limits on time or energies. Yet, although we are cognitively aware of the need for structure, we often psychologicallly permit the light of cooperative communion to flicker beyond its useful life. The fact remains: designing an organized production system requires a formal organization; or to again quote our sage technologist, cooperation alone definitely "won't cut it." We need to know what is expected of us (quantity and quality), to whom we report, and to whom we must relate—and those essential ingredients of effective human interaction are mapped-out by formal organization.

Informal Interpersonal Relationships

The subtleties of informal organizational life become more vivid to those who have experienced behavior in a simulated design department—values, norms, and role expectations, peer pressure, social control, boundary disputes, cooperation, conflict, and compromise all come into finer focus. The typical observations that follow illustrate certain behavioral dimensions that form:

"We couldn't depend on informal splinters from the organization." . "Peer group pressure can have both good and bad effects." . "The pressure from within the individual/subsystems/ groups and from other/subsystems/groups to accomplish the job was *really* felt." . "Personal conflicts showed up very quickly—power plays." . "Great experience in group interaction on both the intellectual and emotional levels."

"The pushing and pulling—receiving and giving—of a production design operation. Even when you think your idea is best, you must compromise for the good of the whole." . "I realized the need to integrate ideas with others *before* coming to a conclusion."

With the opportunity to interact closely with others in a simulated situation, we grasp the chance to analyze other's behavior and our own. Though certain experiences may be mistakenly interpreted, they were at least observed. When these are experienced elsewhere, the observer will perhaps recognize an emerging pattern and search more carefully for causes and solutions.

In sum, real involvement in designing an integrated production system can produce valuable lessons in applying systems theory, formal organization, informal organization, and interpersonal relationships. One participant tidily expressed his impression of the simulation by saying, "More than anything else—I experienced almost every aspect of what we have discussed about socio-technical systems theory."

Summary

To think productively about the design of production systems, one must contemplate managing the systems design effort, for therein lies the perspective, or vantage point, that is sufficiently broad, or suitably comprehensive. This chapter has accordingly placed the reader into the position of a managing design engineer.

We introduced the idea of a "planning department," wherein a design manager is accountable in the final sense for an integrated production system. The design manager's perspective, skills, and role were presented. We then discussed the processes of a simulated design department, its position in the organizational hierarchy, and its responsibilities, constraints, and organizations.

We then turned from the intellectual processes of the simulated design department to a presentation of the conceptual and behavioral insights a person can acquire as a participant. We find that one can witness the application of systems theory to a production problem through heavy involvement. Further, we have found that participants grow more sensitive to the necessities for formal organization, and acquire an awareness of the vicissitudes of their informal interpersonal involvement—all at the visceral level of comprehension.

Notes

1. Leroy H. Mantell, "The Systems Approach and Good Management," *Business Horizons,* (October, 1972), p. 46.
2. David I. Cleland and William R. King, "Developing a Planning Culture for More Effective Strategic Planning," *Long-Range Planning,* (September, 1974).
3. See Chapter 8, "A Strategic Systems Planning Culture," David I. Cleland and William R. King, *Systems Analysis and Project Management,* 2nd ed., (New York: McGraw-Hill Book Company, 1975).
4. David I. Cleland and William R. King, *Systems Analysis and Project Management,* 2nd ed., (New York: McGraw-Hill Book Company, 1975), p. 6.
5. Robert Grandford Wright, *The Nature of Organizations,* (Rancho Palos Verdes, California: Paradigm Publishing Company, 1983), pp. 204–205.
6. Chester I. Barnard, as reported by William B. Wolf in *How to Understand Management,* (Los Angeles, California: Lucas Publishers, 1968) p. 27.
7. John A. Beckett, *Management Dynamics: The New Synthesis,* (New York: McGraw-Hill Book Company, 1971), p. 138.
8. Chester I. Barnard, *The Functions of the Executive,* (Cambridge, Massachusetts: Harvard University Press, 1938), p. 216.
9. Keith Davis and Robert L. Blomstrom, *Business And Its Environment,* (New York: McGraw-Hill Book Company, 1966), pp. 92–93.
10. Wright, *The Nature of Organizations,* pp. 200–201.
11. Based on a faculty working paper by Robert Grandford Wright, "Getting Students Involved With Systems Thinking," No. 73-1, Bureau of Business and Economic Research, Arizona State University.

Chapter VI

Managing The Production System

When we try to pick out anything by itself, we find it hitched to everything else in the universe.[1]

Objectives

This insightful comment was made nearly eighty-five years ago by John Muir, the founder of the Sierra Club. Today, the true meaning of his observation will become clear to the manager of a production system.

The master plan for production is now before the manager. It has been carefully designed to achieve the production goal, through internally consistent and therefore cost effective subsystems, given the time constraints imposed. The manager of the overall production system must now finely calibrate subsystems determined by product configuration to scheduling, physical facilities, purchasing, labor, job design, inventory control, production control, organization, and finally, to costing. This is the *process operation* whereby the capabilities provided by product design and process design are translated to the day-to-day meeting of schedules and standards. Succinctly put, the manager must now ensure that the capabilities designed produce as planned.

Further, the production manager must be prepared to interface with the managers of other subfunctions, such as engineering, marketing, and personnel in the broader organizational system. The manager also will be concerned with influences beyond the boundaries of the organization, in the environmental field, where such things as changes in labor trends and supplier capabilities are felt. Finally, the manager will be intimately involved in renewing the production system as tolerated or dictated by internal or external changes.

Indeed, the manager will quickly learn, as did John Muir years before, that when we try to pick out anything by itself, we find it hitched to everything else. . . ." It would thus be useful to understand what the general manager will experience as he or she directs the production system as it is now designed. The objectives of **Chapter VI** are the following:

- To be aware of the activities and tools necessary to gain system integration
- To know the implications of system interfaces
- To learn the meaning of system renewal.

System Integration

Let us now observe the activities of the general production manager as the final inputs for production conversion are readied. The master plan (Bid Proposal) is implemented in part by securing an appropriate plant facility and capital equipment, stocking raw material inputs, laying out the plant based on job design, and staffing and training production workers. The prescribed hierarchy of the organization emerges with staffing and the technical hierarchy rises with the marshalling of machines, tools, and raw materials. A *socio-technical structure* is created with the capabiity to convert inputs to outputs efficiently.

The structure is now poised to function, but a catalyst is required to transform the structure to a dynamic system. The general manager provides the catalyst, or force, that sparks interrelated activities by delegating authority to the workers throughout the organization. This act gives the workers in all jobs the authority to act, and affixes accountability for production results. The socio-technical structure is thereby transformed into a *socio-technical system*. This is the same process that converted the island castaways in **Appendix III.A** into a social system, but now the technology is far more advanced.

Manager's Self-Concept

The manager recognizes that system design, however well-conceived and well-constructed, will require modifications and adjustments as the production system functions. The design is, after all, a simulation of "the way things should be", recommended by procedures, charts, layouts, and graphs. Its designers could not possibly foresee all the contingencies that now influence actual production, nor was it intended to deal with random disturbances; it is a systems model. But the manager must now deal with such problems.

Out of necessity, the manager's role is that of *efficiency inducer*. He/She wishes to make modifications that will bring on *system calibration*, in order to ensure equilibrium, homeostasis, internal consistency, and efficiency. By efficiency, we mean converting inputs to an optimum number of outputs, given a soundly designed system that uses a minimum of resources for internal self-maintenance.

Manager's Viewpoint

The manager concentrates his or her attention on the overall production system to fulfill the responsibilities implied by the term "efficiency inducer". As the production system comes into focus, the interfaces of the system fade into a hazy, seemingly irrelevant background.

Figure VI.1 illustrates the manager's field of concentration. Here, we see in the Conceptual Overview of a Production Organization that the manager's attention is fixed on those areas shown in bold type. They include the production goals and production organization as they relate to the internal subsystems needed to achieve the goals. At the same time, interfaces with other functions of the overall organization and the broader environment seem inconsequential.

Manager's Tools of Analysis

The manager, acting as *system calibrator,* attempts to preserve stability within the system, minimizing disruptions from any quarter. System maintenance is essential at this phase in the life cycle of the production organization. This condition is required so that activities and processes can be coordinated. Though the system designers provided a potentially powerful "production engine," the final effort to bring it to finely-tuned performance is the mission of the operating manager.

The tools used by the system calibrator to tune the system are the same as those employed earlier by the system designers. The production manager will employ simulation, servomechanisms, critical path analysis, Gantt Charts, runout time calculations, waiting line (queuing) theory, workflows, MRP, job design, and other tools. The manager now also has feedback of *actual* operating data, such as reports on performance from production control, inventory control and quality control, scheduling, labor use, cost breakdowns, equipment maintenance and reliability, scrap, pollution control, and perhaps a computerized information feedback on the overall system's performance. The tools of value engineering, value analysis, work simplification, methods engineering,

Internal Technical Subsystems

Product Configuration
Scheduling
Physical Facilities
Purchasing
Manpower
Job Design
Inventory Control
Quality Control
Production Control
Costing

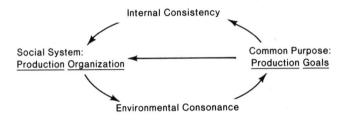

Receptive to Change - Organizational Interfaces

By marketing
By engineering (RID)
By finance
By personnel
By data processing
By top management

Receptive to Change - Outside Interfaces

By customers (consumer taste)
By suppliers (material price)
By employees (new labor contract)
By competitors (new strategy)
By the economy (inflation)
By the government (new regulations)
By technology (new equipment)

Responsive to Forces Urging Change

Able and willing to make effective
changes quickly and economically

Figure VI.1. Conceptual Overview of a Production Organization

preventive maintenance, inventory logistics, variable work schedules, and the reevaluation of production policies and procedures are used to make refinements in the system. The data and tools are used to correct malfunctions and to add refinements. And this activity is a continuing effort.

The manager might observe a backup of work in process due to the ill-timing of inspection at a given point—an internal inconsistency between the subsystems for production control and quality control. The bottleneck will be eliminated by repositioning the check point or the timing of the inspection so that the two schedules are calibrated. Or the manager may adjust the production schedule to accommodate sufficiently high standards of quality. The decision depends on which elements of the problem—positioning, quality level, or timing—are constraints and which elements are variables. If the timing of production is critical and unvarying, it poses a constraint. Thus, the manager will modify the testing point, the rigor of the test, its timing, or some other variable to bring on a balanced flow of work. The manager must be able to distinguish constraints from variables so that malfunctions are removed in a satisfactory way.

The manager will also try to add refinements even if no specific malfunction has been identified. To do so, for instance, the manager may conduct an input/output analysis to find what value might be added to the final product by programmed equipment maintenance or a specific quality inspection technique. This value would of course be relative to the increases in production costs.

The system will be refined further by identifying and eliminating (as best as the manager can) sources of random disturbances to production continuity. In the labor subsystem, for example, the manager may find that random absenteeism or turnover by plant workers intermittently weakens the system and thwarts high production. This random disturbance could cause the manager to arrange for coverages by cross-training workers, engaging back-up workers, or introducing flex-time. Or, if a certain piece of equipment in the critical path of normal production periodically failed, the manager might replace the unit, increase programmed maintenance, install a backup unit, or select alternative paths around the machine.

Whatever the action taken, it is the responsibility of the line production manager to *scan* the operation, sense areas that can be improved, analyze ways to make improvements, select the best alternative, and take the best corrective action for the functioning of the overall system. Malfunctions can thereby be minimized and refinements maximized in both systemic processes and random disturbances.

Managerial:

    leadership styles
    work processes
    authority
    incentives
    control
    formal communications

Behavioral:

    roles, norms, values
    status
    informal interactions
    traditions and customs
    ceremonies, ritual, and symbolism

Technical: (including Economic and Physical)

    product configuration
    scheduling
    physical facilities
    purchasing
    job design
    inventory control
    quality control
    production control
    costing

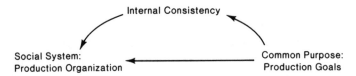

Internal Consistency

Social System: ⟵   Common Purpose:
Production Organization   Production Goals

Figure VI.2. Conceptual Overview Inside a Production Organization Internal Subsystems

Organizational Subsystems

The general manager is not only concerned with the *internal technical subsystem,* as the reader may sense. The manager is concerned with the entire *socio-technical system,* which includes the *technical subsystems,* the *managerial subsystems,* and the *behavioral subsystems.* By re-casting the Conceptual Overview of an Organization (*first introduced in* **Chapter III**) in Figure VI.2, these other elements critical to success can be seen. It seems clear that managing a production system requires a broader awareness and understanding of the nontechnical—managerial and behavioral—subsystems than is required to design the system. Consider the processes of management—planning, organizing, directing, and controlling—presented in **Chapter V,** and the need for broader skills will become apparent. The design process involved planning and organizing only technical arrangements. The management processes, by contrast, require further planning and organizing, but with particular attention to directing and controlling *all* subsystems.

In addition, the manager will become concerned with external influences.

System Interfaces

Up to now, we have presented the production system as a relatively closed system. We drew the conditions of a semi-closed system intentionally to keep the design reasonably simple. The complexities within were quite enough, without compounding the problem with nagging elements demanding attention at the interface of the production system with its environment: no problem with selling the total production run; no products returned by customers for repair, or replacement; no strike by organized labor; no interruption of supplying resources; no energy shortage; no boycott by ecology-minded citizens . . . no external problems. Yet the manager of the system will be beset by certain of these problems at the interface, and others from far too many sources to be able to anticipate fully.

Manager's Self-Concept

The manager must serve as a *systems change agent* to respond to external influencers. This responsiveness is required even though the changes made initially will disrupt the hard-won efficiency that the manager has reached through his role as a *system calibrator.*

Manager's Viewpoint

The manager now focuses attention on the fields upon which the production system depends. The broader organizational system represents immediate interfaces. At these interfaces, for example, engineering may introduce product modifications, top management new

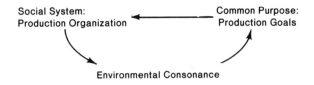

Receptive to Change - Organizational Interfaces

    By marketing
    By engineering (RID)
    By finance
    By personnel
    By data processing
    By top management

Receptive to Change - Outside Interfaces

    By customers (consumer taste)
    By suppliers (material price)
    By employees (new labor contract)
    By competitors (new strategy)
    By the economy (inflation)
    By the government (new regulations)
    By technology (new paper clip design)

Responsive to Forces Urging Change

    Able and willing to make effective
    changes quickly and economically

Figure VI.3. Conceptual Overview Outside a Production System

policies, and data processing new procedures. Beyond the organizational interfaces lies the outside environment of the enterprise. There, for example, the government changes OSHA laws, or pollution emission requirements; an inventor creates an improved machine; or competitors make the inventory of products partially unsalable. The manager's attention is distracted from internal affairs to environmental interfaces, a number of which are depicted in Figure VI.3.

Thus, the manager must be receptive to forces urging change and ready to implement appropriate adjustments if the production system is to be consonant—in phase with—the broader company and its environment. If not, the system will become obsolete. Consider the dilemma of obsolescence one further way. The production system was designed to have sufficient structure to be efficient—technically, managerially, behaviorally. Yet when any structure is unyielding to a field of environmental forces, it will break when pressures attain a sufficient force. For instance, if a product requires modification because of changes in customer's taste, the change can be resisted (probably in the presumed interest of efficiency) until customers find a more satisfying substitute elsewhere. At that time, the resisting production system finds itself in the so-called "buggy whip" business and fails. The manager, therefore, is acutely aware of non-compromising influencers from the field of the production system.

He or she is also cognizant of the ways these forces impinge on the production system initially, and how they reverberate through the subsystems internally. As an example, consider that, as times passes, employees grow to expect more self-management rather than external managing because they become more competent and responsible for their performance. The change in expectations could impinge on the redesign of technical subsystems for job design, scheduling, and the layout of the physical plant. In the managerial subsystem, arrangements for leadership, work processes, use of authority, source of control and communications might be modified. In turn, the behavioral culture within the plant would be transformed. The basis would change for roles, norms, and values, status, informal behavior, and traditions, including ceremonies, rituals, and symbolism. A single change in workers' expectations can sweep through the majority of essential activities. It takes care, competence, and patience to accommodate such a change. Yet if thoroughly done, much of the burden of managing individual workers can be assumed by those who are in the best of all positions to do so. Further, this approach relieves managers from dealing with most of the random deviations in behavior so that they can concentrate on improving the *system*.

A number of environmental interfaces can have far-reaching influences in a similarly pervasive, sequential way. Figure VI.4, a Matrix of Potential Changes by Environmental Forces on Internal Subsystems, provides a classification of changes generated externally and their probable effect on the design of internal arrangements.

Socio-Technical Subsystems

Figure VI.4. A Matrix of Potential Changes by Environmental Forces on Internal Subsystems

Environmental Interfaces	Technical							Managerial						Behavioral			
	Product Scheduling	Physical Facilities	Purchasing	Major Job Design	Inventory Control	Product Control/Quality	Costing	Styles	Work Processes	Authority	Incentives	Communications	Role Values/Norms	Status	Interaction	Ceremonials	Symbolism
Organizational																	
Marketing	X	X	X	X	X		X	X	X		X	X		X	X		
Engineering	X	X	X	X	X	X	X	X	X		X	X	X	X	X	X	X
Finance			X				X	X	X		X	X					
Personnel	X			X	X	X	X	X	X	X	X	X	X	X	X	X	
Data Processing	X		X	X	X	X	X	X	X	X	X	X	X	X	X	X	X
Outside																	
Customers	X		X	X	X	X	X	X						X			
Suppliers	X	X	X		X		X	X	X	X	X	X	X		X		X
Employees	X	X		X		X	X	X	X	X	X	X		X	X	X	X
Competitors	X	X	X		X	X	X										
Economy	X	X	X	X	X		X	X	X	X	X	X		X	X	X	
Government	X	X	X	X		X	X	X	X	X	X	X	X	X	X	X	
Technology	X	X	X	X	X	X	X	X	X	X	X	X	X	X	X	X	X

Manager's Tools of Analysis

All production systems are confronted by changes from their environments. These changes cause problems of accommodation, but they also open opportunities. The change of expectations by employees presented earlier, for instance, caused widespread modifications of on-going subsystems. The modifications allowed the workers to relieve management of some of its traditionally burdensome responsibilities, heightened worker identification with the mission of production, and perhaps (just perhaps) instilled a deeper dedication to excellent performance.

The central analytical tool needed to respond appropriately to environmental change is an awareness of open systems theory. That theory is reviewed here as it applies directly to production systems. A second consideration for the general production manager is redesigning the production system to respond to a change outside, assuming that there are several options available. Here, we are reconsidering the influence of equifinality, in which there are a number of ways to accomplish the same goal, or final output. The third major consideration that the production manager ponders is the way the change decided upon should be implemented in the production system.

Open Production Systems Theory

Production systems are viable organisms, not static structures where designed features and activities are irreversibly fixed. There exists an ongoing interface with a fluid field of external forces and a continual interplay with the environment. Specifically, there is a continuous variation of *inputs*—materials, labor, equipment, money, and energies—requiring continuous modifications of the *conversion process,* and periodic changes of products or services produced as *outputs.*

Production systems in the short run also have structural properties that cannot be changed. For instance, a major machine cannot be replaced overnight, limits on the availability of certain skilled workers may restrict expansion, or the bounds on technical know-how can impede new applications. These structures, among others, act as constraints or parameters that prevent change in the short run. Other production properties can be changed quickly, as variables. The manager can discern what can be changed (*variables*) and what cannot be changed (*constraints*). The manager is also aware of properties that can be adjusted quickly (*short-run*) as contrasted to those requiring substantial lead time (*long-run*) to change. Thus, a production system is indeed open to sweeping changes over time (full metamorphosis) but in day-to-day short term decisions it is bounded (partial adaptations) by structural constraints.

The manager of the production system is conscious of the factors that cause the system to lose force or run down, a flaw inherent in all open systems. This, you may recall, is termed *negative entropy*. It can occur by drawing more resources from the environment than is directly reflected in output. As one example, it is tempting to over-supply materials to decrease the risk of outages. Doing so beyond a well-chosen point, however, drains the system by tying-up capital, space, and maintenance. As another example, when money and work-hours are made available, they may be used to increase equipment maintenance to a degree that is imprudently high, to protect machine investments and to assure continuous use. As a final more discrete example of negative entropy, recall that systems use resources for output and *self-maintenance*. When a system uses an inordinately high amount of resources to merely maintain the system, output diminishes. It runs down. A production system can overly emphasize its own maintenance easily by over-staffing (especially in the management positions), over-reporting activities, or over-proceduralizing the events and activities necessary to produce something of value. The professional operating manager is alert to symptoms that signal negative entropy. The manager is also sensitive to factors from the environment that can infuse the system with positive momentum. These stimuli might include new technology, advanced conversion methods, work simplification approaches, or work grouping innovations. Whatever the thrust or origin of these stimuli, the enlightened manager is willing to consider their potential to slow, arrest, or reverse entropy. *Negative and positive feedback* from outside the production system are required to remain current and sound. The manager will be guided by *negative feedback,* such as consumer concern about the durability of the product that may signal the need for higher standards. Unfortunately, most systems are managed predominantly on negative feedback. Stated another way, "management by exception"—the idea that exceptions from desirable performance are those things that are managed—has evolved to mean "manage by negative exception." The behaviorally astute manager also uses *positive feedback* to benefit the system. The manager may learn from the personnel office, for example, that exit interviews reveal that employees leave to advance their careers only when opportunities within limit professional growth. The evidence guides the manager to recognize the sources of high morale, to preserve healthful interpersonal relations, and perhaps to design "career ladders" within the system and the broader company.

Programs are designed to ensure that feedback, or inputs of relevant information, flow into the production system. A program also suggests how the data is used. As examples, programs should be set procedurally to get information on labor statistics, personal consumer preferences from marketing research, and the cost of capital from finance. The program will also establish who gets the data within the production system, the decisions that have to be made, and the action to be taken.

The production system is modified and thereby adapted to forces from its varied interfaces that make it more internally efficient or more consonant with the environment outside. The production manager is mindful to resist unnecessary changes that only disrupt the continuity of the process, and receptive to required or desirable changes. The key is to preserve the integrity of an internally consistent system while adapting it for environmental consonance—this is called maintaining *dynamic equilibrium.*

The Adaptive Process

Enlightened managers of production systems often assign individuals or special units of people to the primary job of monitoring feedback and translating it into action plans for adaptation. Then when a significant change in the environment is anticipated or observed by feedback, it becomes a part of the program analyzed by the person(s) responsible initially for Production System Planning, operations research, or whatever it is called. Using decision theory, cost-effectiveness analysis, and other techniques, the specialist in planning, in cooperation with outside organizational functional units, recommends an adaptive strategy to the production manager. The manager then approves and implements the strategy if it appears sound.

Implementing Change

The production manager's first concern is that the adoption does not create systemic inconsistencies that drain the force of the system and cause a particularly flagrant variety of negative entropy. The design of the adaptive modification is first checked against goals and all technical subsystems to ensure calibration after the modification is operationalized. It is then checked against managerial subsystems to ensure, for

Internal Subsystems
(Hierarchy of Plans)

Technical:
    product configuration
    scheduling
    physical facilities
    purchasing
    job design
    inventory control
    quality control
    production control
    costing

Managerial:
    leadership styles
    work processes
    authority
    incentives
    control
    formal communications

Behavioral:
    roles, norms, values
    status
    informal interactions
    traditions and customs
    ceremonies, ritual, and symbolism

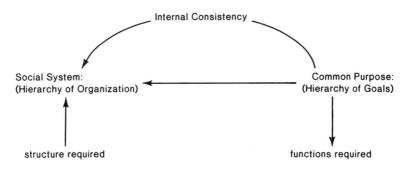

Figure VI.5. Sequential Analysis of Implementing Change

example, that workers have sufficient authority to carry out the tasks modified, that incentives encourage acceptance of the new way, and that the means to control performance are available. The manager finally relates the modification to the on-going behavioral subsystem in effect *among* the people in the plant. The question must be answered: What effect does this change have on the people—their roles, norms, values, interaction, traditions, and especially, *status?* The sequence of our analysis here is portrayed in Figure VI.5.

The production manager can now direct the people to implement the change, since the plan has been checked for consistency throughout. This traditional means of affecting change may back-fire because it makes two bold assumptions: It first assumes that the general manager and planning staff know everything happening in the system with the *people;* and second, that ideas from "outside" the operating level will be warmly accepted and zealously adopted. Neither assumptions have proved to be always true. Probably no one knows all of the subtleties, the behavioral nuances, that influence the human side of the system. Change is scary for all people because it is a harbinger of the unknown. Will it mean layoffs? Will my skills become obsolete? Will I lose respect? And so on. Perhaps there is a sounder way.

Some production managers will look on the "modificatiion plan," though it seems logical, as a *tentative* plan. As such, it will be examined by those people affected by it for refinements, and particularly, reasons for resistance. Worthy ideas will be incorporated into the design and unwarranted reasons for resistance minimized. The final modification plan, as an intellectual/behavioral product of all persons influenced by the change, may be made much "sounder" in that the chances of it being "warmly accepted and zealously adopted" are substantially increased. Though autocratic directives are quick, they are also often "quick and dirty" because full implementation is never fully accepted and psychologically embraced by those who must implement change.

A Departure: Back to General Systems Theory

Near the beginning of our study in **Chapter I,** we considered the meaning of Kenneth Boulding's Hierarchy of System Levels for designing production systems. It is here reproduced as Figure VI.6 to refresh your memory. As you may recall, it reminds us that systems emerge from elementary frameworks, through succeeding levels of compexity and abstraction, to end finally with transcendental systems of the highest conceptual plane.

Further, we are told that all higher level systems include the elements of all systems below them in sophistication. Let's now consider the meaning of this model to production systems designers and production managers. Designers of production systems operate mainly on levels 1 through 4, the technical subsystem—frameworks, clockworks, cybernetics, and open systems—and pay only slight attention to the real human

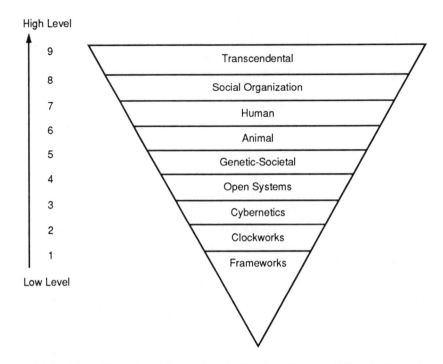

High Level

Low Level

9 Transcendental
8 Social Organization
7 Human
6 Animal
5 Genetic-Societal
4 Open Systems
3 Cybernetics
2 Clockworks
1 Frameworks

Figure VI.6. Hierarchy of System Levels Based on Degrees of Complexity and Abstraction

issues involved in an on-going socio-technical system. Production managers, in contrast, are involved with those lower order concepts, and are also intimately concerned with system levels 7 and 8—human and social organization—because managerial and behavioral subsystems reside therein. These are also crucially important to the overall performance of the production system. This is merely a reminder that managing the system requires that the manager understand systems beyond the technical—and that those essential human and social organization systems are on an advanced plane of knowledge.

System Renewal

Most of us do not design the system we manage. We "inherit" it. We are assigned to an ongoing production function that is a product of certain elements of design, certain agents of historical accident, and certain idiosyncrasies of the people who were part of it. It may have become a "crazy-quilt" of activities and events. Whatever its nature, we are as-signed to improve it. Hence, it seems reasonable that we narrow our in-quiry to renewal of an existing system. The initial step is to recognize systems that are incoherent, that have in some way either become in-ternally inconsistent or lost consonance with their environments. Once ambiguities are identified and recognized as such, men and women in management can correct them. So let's review a few samples of errant systems to warm-up your analytical engines. You already have a model of an efficient production system. Now let's look at some "fictionalized" systems with faults.

The first example, Alpha Airframe, deals with a lack of environ-mental consonance; the second, Beta Aerospace, demonstrates internal inconsistency; and the third example, Omega University, is a fictional account in which a system is fraught with goal ambiguity as it relates to incentives. Here we go.

Alpha Airframe. During the maturing stage of Alpha Airframe, the company became remarkably successful in engineering and con-structing aircraft frames. It was a highly profitable firm, with cost-effective efficient systems for production. Its founder identified the mission of the company as "efficient air frame producers," which was entirely congruent with external demands at that time. In turn, the lead-ership turned its attention inward to continue modifying and refining the production system.

The son of the founder assumed the position of chief executive of-ficer as the company moved into its aging stage. It did so because by internalizing and building-in rigidities, it grew impervious to the outside world that was whirling along. At its interfaces with the external envi-ronment, dramatic changes occurred. Changing technology, political support, and public expectations ushered in jet transport. With the speed and efficiency of jet engines, fewer airframes are needed. Other oppor-tunities were available in the fields of aerospace, missiles, and nuclear powered sea craft. But viewing these changes as opportunities would have required a change of mission from "producers of airframes" to, say, de-signers and processors of aluminum. The leadership was unwilling to redefine the firm's mission, probably because it had been so successful in the past and its leaders were concentrating on internal affairs to the neglect of external interfaces. With its narrowed area of expertise, the company's fate was predestined. It now lacked consonance with envi-ronmental demands.

We can almost hear the president of Alpha proclaiming to the end, "we have been the best airframe producers for two generations, and if it was good business for Dad, it's good business for me." Its demise was marked by obsolescence and failure. Oh yes, what was the final resting place of Alpha? It was merged into the organization of a strong competitor and became known as Gamma-Alpha, Division for Processing Esoteric Metals—or something like that.

Beta Aerospace. Beta designs and produces for space ventures and weapons systems. In time frame one, the company was awarded a contract by NASA to design and produce a prototype of a highly sophisticated piece of space hardware on which astronauts' lives would depend. NASA was particularly conscious of the consequences of failure and insisted that the prototype be as perfect as possible, with backup subsystems available so that the unit would be operationally "fail safe." Since the component was a pioneering effort with no precedence as to cost, NASA granted a cost contract, plus a fixed rate of profit.

The goal—common purpose—was crisply defined, the functions clearly inferred, and the structure of the socio-technical production system designed to reflect the demands of the project. Engineering, skilled production craftsmen, purchasing, and quality control assumed prominence in the system. Precision equipment was acquired. Management subsystems were also designed to encourage professionalism and craftsmanship. Indeed, a major "zero-defects" program became an institutionalized segment of the culture of Beta. Handsome awards were given for innovative engineering, incentives for quality assurance, and rewards for commitment to high standards throughout the system. We note a supportive ritual wherein each employee wears a bold pin, next to the security badge, which exclaims, "PRIDE." All subsystems seem consistent. They support each other, the program, the goal, and Beta Aerospace. Hence, the component is successfully completed.

Beta, in time phase two, has won a contract from the DOD to produce large numbers of small missiles. The letting agency, DOD, has experience in the production of these devices, so cost comparisons were available and tolerances for malfunctions were assessed to be comparably high. The contract was let, thus, on a straight competitive bid basis—not cost-plus profit—and Beta won the contract as the lowest bidder with the capability to fulfill the contract.

Beta Aerospace swung into the new challenge resolutely. With the new goal also fixed, it analyzed functions required and designed them into the socio-technical system. Management systems were reformed to support high productivity, manufacturing took a status advantage over engineering, incentives were given to high volume producers, and "PRIDE" pins grew less fashionable. But costs soared to a dangerously high level because a gross internal inconsistency was permitted to exist. Inexplicably, the "zero-defects" program was retained; it overemphasized quality and sent costs spiraling.

How could such a condition be permitted to exist? In all mature organizations, we find "minor cults" and "major religions." Cults can be questioned, and, if found to be inappropriate, changed. But a major religion is rarely censured. The "zero-defects" program had acquired a sort of spiritual sanctity, because it was an institutionalized process that had once worked. Further, it was guarded by those people who had made it work, believed in it, and had developed vested interests in its continuation. The institution for control thrived; Beta Aerospace languished.

Omega University. Omega U. was constituted with the noblest of missions in mind. In fact, some referred to it fondly as "Utopia U." It really should have been so. You see, it was started by a dedicated group of well-experienced students. (Some had even studied at a university as undergrads for seven or eight years to get a four-year degree.) They had become authorities on higher education while leisurely indulging in intellectual grazing. So they knew what they wanted Omega to stand for. They established themselves as the Board of Regents to assure that the University met the following goals, *in their order of importance:*

1. Teaching, learning, exchanging facts and ideas
2. Physically decentralized for those students, wherever they wish to learn
3. Service to the community (social, political, business, and so on)
4. Advance knowledge, research and publication.

The minor goal of advancing knowledge through research and publication was grudgingly accepted by the Board members. It was admitted only after one regent pointed up that unless teachers are involved in exploring their respective fields, they can become out-of-touch and obsolete.

The goals were set: The design was drawn innovatively based on functions. The library was central. Study areas were grouped along topical lines rather than traditional disciplines so that if a student wished to study production/operations, for example, he or she would find that the module of teachers included such fields as product design, industrial engineering, production technical systems, production managerial systems, and production socio-behavioral systems. Gifted people who adored teaching were attracted from varied sources. Learning centers were established wherever needed. A management subsystem was designed so that authority flowed upward and across; control was delegated to teaching peers; and multi-directional, open communication was encouraged throughout.

But alas, when the Regents got to the incentive subsystem, their design was momentarily halted. What is the basis for giving salary increases, promotions, and honors? Teaching, of course, given our superordinate goals. But what teacher gives the most . . . immediately applicable skills, worldly wisdom, the means for life-long learning, or (gag) merely the most popular? Answer: We don't know. Hence, we must search for an alternative basis for providing incentives. The Regents look back to goals for a clue. Goals 2, decentralizing learning opportunities, and 3, community service, are unmeasurable. Eureka! Goal 4, research and publications, *is* measurable. So it was that the Regents of Omega U. (earlier even affectionately called, "Utopia U.") built their incentives on a minor, "grudgingly accepted" goal, and as a consequence turned a teaching institution into a research center. Research inadvertently became the primary goal. Over time, the entire character of Omega changed in response and the Regents grew to accept the ambiguity of it all as more and more campus buildings were named after them.

A Russian Experience. Failures to renew production processes systematically are in no way culturally specific or politically determined. The problem is universal, especially in nations applying advanced technology. The article presented on the following page is an amusing account of one such experience in the Soviet Union where a lapse of systems thinking caused untold economic waste and human frustration.

Beer-Canning Machinery Gave Soviets a Hangover[2]

MOSCOW—(UPI)—Someone in the Russian Federation Food Ministry probably could use a stiff drink. But please, no beer.

It began in 1969 when a foreign manufacturer brought an automated machine for canning beer to an industrial exhibition in Moscow.

The newspaper Izvestia said the food ministry decided to part with some of its hard currency to buy the machine to use in canning Kvass, a mildly fermented summer drink popular throughout the Soviet Union.

An old production line that annually produced five million liters of beer was dismantled to make way for the new machine.

However, Izvestia said, the new production line "had neither beginning nor end." In other words, the factory had to spend three times as much money on auxiliary equipment to make the thing work.

THIS DONE, the canning process was ready to roll by 1971. One problem: no cans, hence no Kvass.

So a factory in the Ukraine was ordered to produce the necessary containers.

However "out of 7,128 cans filled with Kvass, 7,128 were rejected because it turned out the tinplate couldn't take the pressure," Izvestia said. "And since they weren't properly lacquered inside, the Kvass tasted strange and smelled unpleasant."

Factory directors decided to reduce their product to a gooey concentrate and can that instead.

"IN THE SUMMER of 1973, they prepared to celebrate their total victory over the foreign machinery," Izvestia said. "But instead of the planned capacity of 4,000 cans an hour, the machinery produced 4,782 cans in four months and after that it stopped completely. It seems that equipment constructed to handle liquid couldn't handle thick syrup."

Frustrated, the food ministry imported 600 tons of tinplate and told the factory to go back to the original plan of producing canned Kvass.

But someone apparently forgot that the Soviet Union has no machinery to turn the tinplate into cans.

Finally, the useless production line was dismantled and the various parts of it distributed to factories and stores, Izvestia said.

But that doesn't do much good.

The equipment only works as a whole unit.

Summary of System Renewal. All complex socio-technical systems possess imbalances—some lack of internal or external calibration. They are imperfect. Unlike physical and biological systems designed by laws of nature, production systems are designed and managed by humans and exhibit human nature—strengths and weaknesses.

Yet when the systems essential to a society are permitted to degenerate the condition causes sweeping damages. We will explore the meaning of mismanaged systems in the concluding chapter.

Summary

Designing a production system is a valuable—we believe invaluable—application of system thinking directed primarily at the logical formulation of technical essentials. Managing a production system requires continuing refinements, modifications, and adaptations of the system. In addition to having technical expertise, the line manager must also be astutely aware of the design of managerial and behavioral subsystems. If designers are mostly concerned with the technical arrangements of the socio-technical compound term, then a production manager must emphasize the social arrangements.

System integration is required for efficiency. System interfaces and renewal are essential to long term survival. A production manager must therefore strike a balance between efforts as systems calibrator and system change agent.

The manager will use production systems theory as an analytical framework. Ideas about inputs, conversion, output, constraints, variables, negative and positive feedback, entropy, self-maintenance, and programs will become a way of thinking, and a way of professional life. With these guidelines, the manager's production unit will be managed in a sound state of dynamic equilibrium.

Notes

1. John Muir, undated circular from the Sierra Club.
2. *The Denver Post*, June 23, 1976, p. 33.

Chapter VII

Epilogue

. . . . dreaming of systems so perfect that no one will need to be good.[1]

We come finally to reflect on certain basic questions about designed systems. As with so many studies, when one thinks the end is in sight, it is necessary to go back to the beginning to deal with basic issues. What is a soundly designed system? What isn't a soundly designed system? What are the strengths of sound syytems to individuals and society? What are the inherent weaknesses? And what are the consequences of system failure?

What Production Systems Are and Are Not

Systems are the means to some end. Whether producing products or services, they provide the processes for converting inputs to final outputs. And by that definition, we have included such diverse organizations as General Motors, Bank of America, the YWCA, a job-shop welding shop, or the General Services Administration. Systems are designed based on our knowledge of human beings, technology, and their interface. Since our knowledge is limited, so too is our ability to design systems. Production systems are "artificial systems," as Herbert Simon puts it.[2] As natural systems are based on natural law, socio-technical systems are based on human nature—and are no better, no worse.

Production systems are not based on the dogma of some magical "one best way." Rather, they are based on concepts of situational logic, contingencies, and relativity in a field of changing forces. They are not a Utopian answer to human problems. Mahatma Gandhi was probably correct in speaking critically of those who are ". . . dreaming of systems so perfect that no will need to be good."[3] We hope instead that this book will so heighten the awareness of future system architects that they will be able to *design systems that encourage the expression of the best qualities of men and women*—physical dexterity, curiosity, aesthetics, feelings, or whatever qualities are called for.

It may be that if we are better prepared to design and manage systems, individual participants in systems will be supported in the management of their own behavior. If so, Peter Drucker's optimistic prophecy may become a reality:

> In the long view of history, it is for social innovations—and not technical ones—that America may be best remembered.[4]

In sum, production systems are the logical extensions of our knowledge of models of humans and machines interrelated as means to produce output. Production systems are not panaceas for all human problems. The basic problems will be solved as people grow individually, and as the architects of systems enhance and accommodate that growth.

Indispensable Nature
of Organizational Systems

We are dependent upon formal organizational systems for nearly every enterprise. Beyond our needs for goods and services, human interaction largely fulfills our safety, social, and psychological needs. This observation has been made by a number of authorities, but most directly in satirical form by Burleigh Gardner and David Moore:

> . . . the techniques, processes and structural forms of large-scale organization are here to stay, for it is the primary and basic social invention of civilization. Take away large-scale organization and you are back to living in a cave or mud-hut, eating rutabagas and turnips and discovering why the Anglo-Saxons invented all those four-lettered words, as you try to shoot a racing rabbit with a bow and arrow. It is true that you will no longer be alienated; you will most assuredly be involved; your relation with nature will be intimate and complete. But your concern with that precious little ego of yours and its creative impulse to self-realization will fade into the background, like polite conversation at social teas, as you face the sheer brutality of physical survival.[5]

Organizational systems are essential to people as individuals. They are also indispensable to a strong society:

> The decentralization of power to a myriad of organizations, or pluralism, is unique to democratic societies. The essence of this social phenomenon is basic to all but totalitarian states. Although culture may support the basic ideal of individual freedom, the vigor of any society depends upon the strengths of its organizations. Such critics of democracy and pluralism, as Jose Ortega y Gasset and Wilhelm Röpke[6] warned that a multitude of weak organizations would lead to the demise of a social order. This threat to social integrity is, of course, present to some degree in all societies. However, when a society is dependent upon organizations—standing between the state and the individual for supplying nearly all of the people's needs, strong ones are indispensable.[7]

If all of society's organizational systems, indeed, were somehow dissolved overnight, leaving a massive unstructured group of people to fend for themselves, restructuring would also begin overnight. Such is the indispensability of systems to civilization.

The Weaknesses
of Organizational Systems

Designers of organizational systems, at times, disregard the integrity of human beings who must somehow function within the system, or use obsolete, inadequate, or inaccurate models of what men and women are all about. The systems contrived, as a consequence, overly specialize jobs and methods so that work is dehumanized. Some place such exacting and detailed constraints on certain jobs that there is no room for the worker to *interpret* the role he or she is hired to play. Thus, the worker is stripped of individuality and reduced to an automaton-like state. This form of dehumanizing usually occurs at the lower levels of the system, since managers are supposed to have sufficient discretionary freedom to keep themselves whole in their positions. Further, organizational systems can be designed with so much attention to machine requirements that they neglect human requirements. This form of neglect is particularly prevalent in production systems. Machine requirements are often predominant. Once they are installed, one can somehow find people who will "fit" the technical system (even though the operator should be eight feet tall with three hands to accommodate the design of the machine). Though this tendency has been with us since the Industrial Revolution, we also see it today. (Picture a conversion to computers, and you may sense the organizational or procedural modifications required for the care and feeding of a machine.) Finally, the greater the level of bureaucratizing in the organization, the less need there is for humans to think or to contribute.

Such flaws in organizational systems provoked the late Professor Ralph Linton to make the following observation:

> Since humans are the most intelligent and also the most easily taught of animals, one would expect them to be the most highly individuated. No two persons are exactly alike in their physical and mental potentialities, and certainly no two individuals, even identical twins reared in the same family, have the same experiences. Human beings are thus potentially less alike than the individuals of any other species. It is most surprising therefore, that they have chosen to live in closely organized groups whose members carry on a variety of specialized activities but are mutually interdependent for the satisfaction of practically all their fundamental needs. Many other mammalian species live in herds or packs, but the organization in these is minimal. The only division of activities is that devolving upon the two sexes by their different roles in connection with reproduction, while social control is a simple matter of the poorer fighters giving precedence to the better ones. To find anything which even remotely resembles the complexity of human societies, one must go to the social insects, such as the ants and bees. Here the cooperation which is necessary for the survival of the community is assured by the physical specialization of the various groups of workers, fighters, and so forth, and by a high development of instincts. Since humans lack such instincts, it becomes necessary to subject them to an extraordinarily long and elaborate training if they are to function successfully as members of a society. We are, in fact, anthropoid apes trying to live like termites, and, as any philosophical observer can attest, not doing too well at it.[8]

Certainly, Linton's appraisal is true if organizational systems are designed and managed based upon models that resemble those of the social insects, rather than upon current, adequate, accurate models of social human beings.

System Failures:
An Illustration of the Impact on a Person

Consider finally the plight of an individual subjected to systems that fail us. The treatment of the person is caused systemically, not by random disruptive disturbances. Our hero, used for illustrative purposes here, is a production worker—a part of the system. The impact, of course, could be felt by any one of us. Let's call him, Lester Johnson Morton,[9] an assembler in an automobile plant. Let's observe the influence on Lester caused by errant systems as he lives his life as a worker, a profit-sharer, a user of products and services, and a citizen.

As a Worker. Lester Morton arrives at the plant earlier than usual. For some reason the traffic on the freeway was light and the car didn't overheat. He kills time by going to the cafeteria for coffee. As he stands in line, Lester finds it irritating that it takes as much time to get a cup of coffee as it does to get a five-course meal.

He's on the shift now. The work requires no thought. A chimpanzee could do the task if you could keep it from getting bored and causing trouble, he mused. Careful. Don't get involved. Stay cool. Let your imagination run. It's reflection time:

ON WALKING THROUGH THE GATE[10]

Easy, tedious work—
50 thousand ashtray doors and
100 thousand screws!
Childish, foolish, serious banter
As monotonous as the line—
Are these men—and women—
These workers of the world?
Or is it an overgrown nursery—
This factory—this automobile mill—
With children—goosing, slapping
boys, giggling, snotty girls—
And the teacher with white shirt and
   tie.
40 rules to uphold, the power
To suspend or expel—
"Whistle to whistle you work.
No horseplay—This shit's got to
   stop—"

What is it about that entrance-way,
Those gates to the plant? Is it
The guards—the showing of
Your Badge—the smell?
Is there some invisible eye
That pierces you through and
Transforms your being? Some
Aura or ether, that brain and
Spirit washes you and commands,
"For eight hours now you shall be
   different."
What is it that instantaneously makes
   a child out of a man?
Moments before he was a father, a
   husband, an owner of property,
A voter, a lover, an adult.
When he spoke at least some listened.
Salesmen courted his favors.

Insurance men appealed to his family responsibility.
And, by chance, his church sought his help,
The PTA his support, the United Fund his participation,
The Legion his opinion.
He was calm, refined, mature.
But that was before he shuffled past the guard,
Climbed the steps,
Hung up his coat, and
Took his place along the line.
50 THOUSAND ASHTRAY
DOORS AND
100 THOUSAND SCREWS.
The austere general foreman marches by, his sober eyes seeing all.
The whistle blows, the day shift gleefully plunges for the time clock towards which with guilty glances at the foreman they have been furtively edging for the last 45 seconds.
The line continues inexorably to wind amid a chaotic yet reasoned morass of air hoses, racks, drawers, trash barrels, boxes, screws, stock, and human beings.
The adventures since yesterday are recounted.
Then a pause. Then the clowns take over.
It's goose your buddy time. It's hand wrestling time.
It's argue about who passed the gun down and who didn't time.
It's history of sexual exploits time. It's flip coins time.
It's break time. It's showdown poker time.

It's look at the sunset time.
It's Chevrolet vs. Ford time. It's threat of a drag race time.
It's screw-you time. It's play the numbers time.
It's what's wrong with the Tigers time.
It's lunch time.
It's what the hell's the foreman up to time.
It's rumor time. It's check-pool time.
It's what would I do if they laid me off time.
It's Cadillac is better than Chrysler time.
It's screw the union, screw the company time.
It's look at the women time.
It's lay plans for changeover time.
It's break time.
It's goddam my legs are tired time.
It's someday I'll get out of this goddam factory time.
It's the hell you will, you'll be here till you die time.
It's complain about your wife time.
It's puzzle about your two-year-old time.
It's dream about the sweepstakes time.
It's buy me a coffee time.
It's work ahead so we can get the hell out of here quick time.
It's sneak toward the clock time. It's quitting time.
It's show your lunch box to the guard.
A squeal of rubber, a cloud of dust, and Hyde becomes Jeckyll.
1088–825 becomes Lester Johnson Morton, citizen-husband-father.

As a Profit-Sharer. Driving home, Lester glances down from the road at his annual profit-sharing check. "Peanuts," is the first thought that flits through his mind. Little wonder. All around the plant he sees waste—parts, products, machines, and people. Especially people, he concludes. He's reminded of the power drill left in the wheel well, the bolts left out of the fender, and those industrial injuries that are far removed from "industry." He pictures Charlie Perkins who, as automobile elevator operator, has a job nearly as boring as his. Day after day he takes cars by elevator from one level in the production process to the next. And at certain points in time old Charlie would drop a car—out of sheer boredom, anonymity, and alienation. Lester felt that he should tell someone. But "they" were not receptive to bad news. Anyway, he reasoned that he had to work with these people and to squeal on them would be about as healthy as doing so in prison. He smiled ironically, but with self-satisfaction as he muttered to himself, "that's a pretty close comparison."

Lester glances at the amount of the check again, and concludes finally, "Peanuts!" No wonder it's so small. The assembly-line is set by the engineers to run at a certain speed—not based on workers' speed so much as on the tolerances of the heavy machines. Then, we're asked to compete when we are dependent on others and should cooperate. The general foreman urges us to "work harder," but I wonder if we couldn't work *smarter*. It's damned difficult to want to work faster or smarter when you're paid by the hour to simply be there doing something. What a waste. Frustrating.

Lester's thoughts are interrupted as the freeway system's traffic grinds to a halt. With his car overheating, he exits at the nearest off-ramp and takes to the surface streets. Better. Yet he is always frustrated when he keeps the car moving at the legal speed and finds the traffic lights timed so that he must stop repeatedly. Must be done to issue tickets, he concludes, but how frustrating.

As a Consumer. As the faltering journey home continues, Lester has several errands to perform: The first, to get a present for his wife; the second, to pick up dinner from a take-out place. He wheels into the crowded parking lot of a shopping center and, finding a remote parking place, heads on foot for a retail store.

A hairsetter kit, that's what Lester's wife wants. Hope I can get help on this one. Where are the clerks? Here's one, but she's busy "cashing-out" the register, and there's another taking inventory. Well, he laments, I'll take one and return it if it's wrong. After standing in line to pay, he is directed to another line to have the gift wrapped. He asks for the warranty on the kit and is referred back to the "sales" floor where everyone is busy with everything except customers. "Wonder why that counter was marked 'CUSTOMER SERVICE,'" he asks himself. Gad. Is there any customer service?

On to the Blue Bird Cafe to pick up dinner. Lester is welcomed warmly by signs: "The Management has the Right to Refuse Service to *Anyone,*" "Absolutely, *no* checks cashed," "No substitutes." The staff includes the owner-manager-fry cook, a "seasoned" waitress with the best stations, a junior waitress at the counter, and a bus-boy. What structure, he observed. Hierarchically and procedurally as bureaucratic as the Department of Agriculture. Strange that such a small place can be so rigid, Lester thought. "Say, on that order, can I substitute cottage cheese for potato salad?" He leaves believing that spending one's money is almost as difficult as the job needed to make it.

As a Citizen. Arriving home, Lester is frightened to see that he has again received mail from the Internal Revenue Service. He recalls that he had received a computer printout stating that he owed two dollars more on income taxes filed three years ago. He had written a letter of explanation, then filled-out exacting, detailed forms, and finally, sent IRS a check for the amount in question. Now, what do they want? He tears open the envelope and finds—of all things—a refund check for the originally disputed amount. He is incredulous.

Lester turns his attention to the evening national news. He learns to his dismay that inflation and unemployment can co-exist in an economic system stultified by rigidities, the legal system is delinquent and obsolete, the social security system is going bankrupt, and the postal system needs more funds.

In response to such a concert of failing systems, a person might rush to the window, thrust it open, and shout, "I'm mad as hell, and I'm not going to take it anymore!"[11] And this anger might be particularly intense if the person sensed that there *are* better ways. . . .

Notes

1. Quote from Mahatma Gandhi in E. F. Schumacher's *Small Is Beautiful* (Harper and Row Publishers: New York, 1973), p. 24.
2. Herbert A. Simon, *The Sciences of the Artificial* (Cambridge, Massachusetts: The M.I.T. Press, 1974).
3. Schumacher, *op. cit.*
4. Peter Drucker, *America's Next Twenty Years* (New York: Harper and Brothers, 1955), pp. 15–16.
5. Burliegh B. Gardner and David G. Moore, *Human Relations in Industry* (Homewood, Illinois: Irwin Publishing Co., 1964), p. 16.
6. José Ortega y Gasset, *La Rebelion de las Masas* (Publisher left anonymous at author's request, 1930); and Wilhelm Röpke, *Jenseits von Angebot und Nachfrage,* (unknown).

7. Robert Grandford Wright, *The Nature of Organizations,* (Rancho Palos Verdes, California: Paradigm Publishing Company, 1983), p. 1.
8. Ralph Linton, *The Tree of Culture* (New York: Alford A. Knopf, 1957), p. 11.
9. Adopted from JMC's poem, "On Walking Through the Gate", Life and Work, *Detroit Industrial Mission,* Vol. 14, No. 4, Winter 1974.
10. *Ibid.*
11. NETWORK, a film released in 1976 by M.G.M.

Index

Production management, 27
Production manager, 127
Production organization, 128, 130
Production organization internal subsystems, 130
Production plants, 53
Production policies, 129
Production systems
    complexity of, 105
    comprehending, 85
    conceptual overview of, 132
    control of, 129
    elements of, 96–97
    inputs for, 103
    integrated of, 126
    interface, 131–142
    management of, 125–147
    model of, 30
    nature, 93–104
    overall, 31
    overview of, 132
    renewal, 140
    resources, 98
    stocks and flows of, 103
    structures of, 97–98
    theory, 135–136
    understanding, 85
Productivity, 69, 101
Product specialists, 92
Profit-sharer, 152
Profit sharing, 30
Programs, 37, 137
Progressive organizations, 109
Projects, 37, 109
Project teams, 109
Public expectations, 141
Public opinion, 25, 46
Public relations, 93
Purchasing, 98, 102–103, 118, 125, 130, 138
Purchasing subsystems, 111

Q

Qualitative rewards, 30
Quantitative rewards, 30
Quality control
    data for, 127
    factors of, 102
    implementing, 138
    in metals, 92
    input for, 102–103
    monitoring, 31, 127
    priority, 50
    production and, 92
    subsystems for, 34, 102, 118, 129–130

R

Rate of flow, 104
Raw materials, 19, 68, 93, 98–99, 102, 104
Real-time information systems, 54
Reasoning process, 65
Reasons for development, 11
Relevant zones, 88, 98
Request for bid memo, 117
Requirements of organized life, 48
Research laboratories, 25
Resources, 98
Retooling, 33
Rightful power, 61
Rigidity, 80
Roles, 113, 130, 138
Rules, 67
Runout time calculations, 127

S

Safety, 71, 93, 111
Satellites, 20
Scheduling, 31, 99, 102–103, 118, 125, 130, 138
Scrap, 127
Screws, 98
Self-determination, 122
Self-maintenance, 69
Sensitivity training, 54
Sequential analysis of implementing change, 138
Servomechanisms, 127
Servosystem models, 31
Servosystems, 29, 31, 102
Sewing, 102
Shaping, 100, 102
Shaping tubing, 102
Simulated design department, 120
Size of stock, 104
Skills, 112
Social order, 149
Social organizations, 19
Social systems, 49, 58, 65
Socio-technical systems
    designing, 1, 38
    special type of system, 38
    subsystems, 134
    systems, 107
Sources of inefficiency, 64
Space colony, 20
Spacecraft, 31
Specialization, 62
Specialized staffs, 42
Stability, 8
Staff advisors, 75
Staff specialists, 99